Rum Jungle

Rum Jungle

BY ALAN MOOREHEAD

1954

CHARLES SCRIBNER'S SONS

NEW YORK

Title-page drawing by

FRANK WILIMCZYK

TO
RICHARD

CONTENTS

ILLUSTRATIONS

Rum Jungle

CHAPTER ONE

A Nameless, Hopeless Distress

THERE are no lost cities in Australia. Apart from the
blackfellows there is no evidence that any civilization
ever existed there until the end of the eighteenth century,
when the first white settlers arrived from England. They
came round the Cape of Good Hope by sailing ship, a six-
months' journey, and they might just as well have been
going to the moon, they were so irrevocably cut off from
the rest of the world and everything they had known and
lived for up till then. Most of them were convicts who were
condemned to exile for the term of their natural lives.
Later on, when gold was discovered in the eighteen-fifties,
others came out of their own accord, but for them too it
was a drastic break with their past lives; very few of them
had any prospect of getting back to Europe again. It was
a much greater step than the Pilgrim Fathers took when
they left Europe: America lay in the same hemisphere and
was only two or three thousand miles away. The journey
to Australia was some 15,000 miles, endless uncharted
seas and countries lay in between, and there was nothing
in Australia to help the new settlers to establish themselves; it was a wilderness. Like Robinson Crusoe they
had to start again from the beginning.

In the intervening years since then a thousand things
have arrived to complicate the scene, but this is the root
instinct in the Australian mind, a sense of isolation, and
anyone who is born there is sure to feel it, though perhaps
unconsciously, no matter where he goes or what he does.

For the early settlers it was, in fact, a double isolation: they had not only lost Europe but they failed to occupy the new continent. It was too big, too inhospitable. They perched themselves on the extreme fringe of the country, on the south-eastern coast, like visitors in the outward rooms of a vast empty house; and so, to some extent, they were isolated from Australia itself. Like a colony of ants that is suddenly removed from one place to another these first pioneers took the only course that was open to them; they set about establishing a civilization which was as faithful a copy of everything they had left behind in England as they could make it; and this is why Australia is such an odd country. It is a piece of the bourgeoisie dumped down in the Pacific. As far as possible the local environment was ignored; all things had to be a reflection of life in England, the clothes they wore, the food they ate, the language, the sports, the music, the books and, most of all, the common law. None of it was native. Everything was imported. And because they believed that the imitation could never be as good as the original, they were afflicted always with a feeling of nostalgia, a yearning to go back to their lost homes on the other side of the world. They tried to cover it up with an outward show of independence but nevertheless it was there.

I was a third-generation Australian and at the time I arrived on the scene in 1910 all these reflected English manners and customs were surviving strongly. England was never referred to as England, but simply as 'Home'. The English Christmas falls in midwinter while in Australia it is broiling midsummer. But that made no difference to us. In a temperature that was often well over 100 degrees in the shade we sat down to an overpowering Christmas dinner of turkey and plum-pudding (with a sprig of English holly on the top), and when we smaller children had eaten to the point of bursting we grew purple in the face and were afflicted with the most violent pangs brought on by indigestion, excitement, and the heat. To this day I always associate Christmas with being sick.

Our religious services were Presbyterian or Church of England and of an appalling dullness. Our schools were imitations of English and Scottish schools, with English books and imported English masters. Our lighter reading was *Chums* and the *Boys' Own Paper*, *Magnet*, and comics printed in England; then, as we got older, *Punch*, the *London Illustrated News*, and a batch of other magazines that have all vanished now: *Pearson's*, *Nash's*, *Pall Mall*, the *Windsor*, the *Royal*, and the *Strand*. We had a holiday on the King's birthday; the King himself (George V) almost as remote and awesome as God, but still my king; and we sang lustily at the end of the school concerts:

> *God save our gracious King,*
> *Send him victorious*
> *Long to reign over us*
> *God save our King.*

Whenever England went to war, we, 15,000 miles away, went to war too, and on Armistice Day, some twelve hours ahead of the rest of the world, we stood for two minutes' silence.

I cannot remember ever seeing a blackfellow while I was at school, although of course we knew 'the abos' were somewhere there in the bush and we treated them as a great joke. Certainly we knew nothing of their language or their customs—those things were all rather debased. Our way ahead lay through bright concrete buildings, new roads, and motor-cars, and the latest fashion magazine from Europe. We were all very proud of Madame Melba, who had gone abroad and shown what an Australian could do at Covent Garden, at La Scala, and the Metropolitan. And we were even more proud of our cricketers and tennis players when they won at Lords and at Wimbledon.

To go abroad—that was the thing. That was the way

to make your name. To stay at home was to condemn
yourself to nonentity. Success depended upon an imprima-
tur from London, and it did not matter whether you were
a surgeon, a writer, a banker, or a politician; to be really
someone in Australian eyes you first had to make your mark
or win your degree on the other side of the world.

There were, of course, quite a number of mannerisms
and customs which were forced upon us by the Australian
climate, the soil, and the isolation, but I never recognized
them as such; I thought they were all basically English.
There was the Australian accent. People living in England
were supposed to have slightly affected but rather nice
'speaking voices'. But, as a boy, I never thought there was
any marked difference in the way they spoke; I assumed
broadly that all English people spoke as I did, with a
cockney accent, and I would have been mortified if anyone
had said that I had any accent at all. The Americans were
different. There was an accent for you, and very funny it
was. Didn't they know that 'jarb' was spelt job, and that
an ant was a small insect, not a female relative? We used
to imitate the Yankee accent with much drollery at school
and it was perhaps fortunate that we were not aware that
when such words as 'basin' and 'place' fell from our gentle
lips they turned out to be 'bison' and 'plice'. We knew
such lines as 'What are the wild waves saying?' as well
as any little boy at Eton, and what did it matter that it
sounded like, 'What are the wild wives sighing?'—that
was the way you said it.

Equally I assumed that everyone in the Empire (that is
to say, every *white* man, the coloured people were hopeless) took a shower (not a bath) first thing in the morning,
as I did, and then proceeded to a breakfast of strong tea
and chops or steak. Dinner, a mammoth meal, consisting of
a hot joint, vegetables, a pudding, and more tea, was
usually eaten in the middle of the day, and the evening
meal, always known simply as 'tea', was taken at six p.m.

or perhaps at six-thirty, never later. It usually meant more
meat and more tea. 'Afternoon tea' was a quite separate
operation; that was the couple of cups you had with a wedge
of fruit cake in the middle of the afternoon. All these prac-
tices I accepted as part of the universal and immovable
order of things.

In the same way I took it for granted that for all social
occasions, at any time of the day or night, beer was the
drink. You did not take it with your meals but before or
afterwards and in considerable quantities. Beer was the
solace of life and the white man's true vision of bliss. You
drank it, either at home in pint bottles, or standing up in
a bar (from which all women were excluded) in thick glass
pots. And since beer exercised so potent a spell and was so
delectable in every way, it was only natural that all public
houses should close at six in the evening and that the sale
of all alcoholic liquor should be prevented by law until
nine o'clock the following morning. On Sunday the pubs
were closed altogether. Had men been able to drink at
leisure at any time of the day or night there was no saying
what they would do: that was the underlying fear.

I don't believe that my elders relished these strange
licensing laws any more than they do now, but they had
become the established custom, they defined, as it were,
the hours of permissible vice, and the stars in their courses
were not more regular than the scene that was repeated
every day in every city street at five o'clock. That was the
moment when the whistle blew, the factories and the
offices stopped work, and the men came hurrying in thousands to the pubs to make the best of the one remaining
hour of legal drinking. You drank standing up. It was
quicker that way. The drinking of wine during meals, or
indeed the use of any alcoholic liquor as a leisurely and not
necessarily evil thing, designed to stimulate friendly social
intercourse between men and women, had not at this stage
come into my experience.

Innocent pleasure was something quite different and it was concerned almost entirely with sport. Cricket and football were, of course, the ruling passions and we all played them constantly. But it would have seemed monstrous to me if every summer we did not spend at least a month by the sea on a wide beach of yellow sand. Everyone I knew did that, and usually you could count on three or four months' swimming in the year. We swam as we walked, as a simple matter of course. We surfed in the long breakers coming in from the Pacific, and by the end of every summer we were sunburnt to a shade of deep mahogany. Sundays were usually the time for tennis, and Sunday evenings, in our not so religious family, the time for cards. We played euchre, whist, and auction bridge; and this was interspersed with ping-pong and dancing to a hand-cranked gramophone which always stood in one corner of the room, with a cardboard horn that emerged from the sound-box like a vast tropical flower. There was just one broadcasting station called 3 LO and every boy constructed for himself a 'receiving set'; it consisted usually of a rickety collection of coils and wires in a cigar-box, and one sat there, sometimes for hours on end, ear-phones clamped to the head, poking at a piece of crystal with a thin antenna of wire. If you touched the right spot on the crystal the baritone from 3 LO came through loud and clear:

> *Sons of the sea-hee*
> *All British bor-orn;*

if not, you got a horrible screeching, more dreadful than the sighing of wild wives or the screams of the banshee which, I imagined, lived up the chimney in the winter nights.

Television and 'the talkies' were, of course, unheard of, but we were taken occasionally to the local picture palace to see Charlie Chaplin, Sessue Hayakawa, the Japanese actor, Lilian Gish (whom I hated), and William S. Hart, the leathery hero of a thousand headlong rides across the purple sage. Each Christmas we went to *Puss in Boots*, *Cinderella*, or one of the other pantomimes (this was a sturdy English survival), and Wirth's Circus; but the legitimate theatre was a rare event unless it was Allan Wilkie and Miss Hunter-Watts playing Shakespeare, or Miss Gladys Moncrieff, Australia's own soprano, in the operetta *The Maid of the Mountains*. Actually there were more stage shows in Sydney and Melbourne then than there are now, and I seem to remember a music-hall called The Bijou, a place of the earthiest kind of humour; but it was never mentioned at home and I had to go to it surreptitiously one Saturday afternoon, with a friend who provided the shilling for two seats in the gods.

We had a slang of our own and some of it still survives: something good was 'beaut' or 'bonza', something bad was, as in France, 'a cow'. When my mother went to a party she called it a 'chevoo'—presumably from the French *chez vous*—and the phrase for an emphatic agreement was always 'too right'. Swear words like 'bloody' and 'bastard' were worked to death. Nearly all Australian slang can be traced to its origins very easily but the accent itself remains a mystery and I have never heard it satisfactorily explained. Only a very few of the first settlers were cockneys, and in any case the cockney accent is the product of the smoke and the fogs of London, an entirely different climate to Australia. One might more easily have expected it in New Zealand, which is a colder place, but New Zealanders have very little accent at all.

Foreign languages we never heard from one year's end to another except for a little anglicized French at school, and indeed few foreigners ever came to Australia. Right up to the end of the First World War (when I was eight), and even much later Australians, were probably the purest English-Scottish-Irish stock in the world, a good deal purer than the stock of the United Kingdom itself. There were a few Germans in South Australia, a few Italians on the sugar-cane fields in Queensland, and every town had a little group of Chinese who ran the laundries and the market gardens—but that was all. The White Australia policy was the sacred cornerstone of our existence. We felt that if we ever relaxed it for an instant the teeming millions of the East would at once light down upon us like some Biblical plague. If a coloured man tried to enter the country he was excluded by a very simple device: the language test. He would be asked to translate some fifty words of a language that was not his own—and the port officials made sure that it was a language which he could not conceivably know. Once, I remember, there was a great stir when the Commonwealth Government wished to exclude a Central European writer who was suspected of being a communist. He was given a passage of Gaelic to translate, and being a fabulous linguist he translated it at once, and demanded entry. They had to find another legal device to get him out.

On the whole I don't suppose our prejudices were so very much worse or sillier than in other countries, either then or now. Germans were to us, quite simply, monsters (this was during the 1914–18 war), the French were lascivious and sharp, the Italians unreliable and physically rather dirty, the Scandinavians clean but uninteresting, the Dutch clean but gross, the Americans boasters, though fundamentally normal, and the English were 'pommies'. This word 'pommy' was a term of slight derision—it was meant to indicate the la-de-da Englishman in a top hat and a monocle who was already a great figure of fun on the music-halls; but there was no active dislike in it. It never attached to British institutions; no one would ever have dreamed of calling the King a pommy. It was really a defensive term, for the Australian was for ever on the watch for the slightest show of superiority in the English.

This was, of course, not so very different from the American approach, and to the attitude conveyed by the American word 'limey'; but it went a good deal deeper in Australia, for we were British still, incontestably and willingly so. But we had to show our independence. We had built up our own lives here on the other side of the world and nobody was going to lord it over us. In our hearts perhaps we did feel a little inferior, too provincial and unmannered, but we fiercely resented having it pointed out to us. Even among ourselves we took the most elaborate care never to suggest by so much as a word or a gesture that we might be socially or intellectually superior to anybody else. To be 'stuck up', to put on airs—that was the really vital crime and it was stamped on mercilessly. The taxi-driver or the waiter in the hotel was just as good as his client, possibly a good deal better. He would never have called him 'sir'. On the other hand, in those days he would never have taken a tip either.

For the rest I think we were a kindly and hospitable people. Having no inherited wealth we were for ever getting into financial trouble and helping one another. To some extent even the city people felt they were embarked on an adventure in a new and not very fertile land, and when a disaster occurred, a flood, a bush-fire, or a drought, they gave generously. It was a very strong tradition that you should help your neighbour. We lived healthy and simple lives and most children grew up very straight and tall, with an air of the out-of-doors in the way they walked and held themselves. We were the reverse of neurotic, our lives were bound to constant physical activity, and we learned to depend upon ourselves. When the car broke down you mended it yourself. Men went out into the bush, cleared the trees, and built houses and furniture with their own hands. Our attitude was 'let's give it a go', 'let's try and see what happens', and so we were for ever experimenting and taking chances. We never suffered, as

the Europeans did, from ennui, from a feeling that we
were surrounded by entrenched prejudices and rivalries.
In Europe everything had been done a thousand times
before; in Australia all things were new. And there were
not many government prescriptions and regulations. Certainly we never heard of rationing. I grew up believing
that anything was possible—I could become a general or
a jockey, a poet or a multi-millionaire.

And yet I do not believe I was very happy. As far back
as I can remember I was dogged by a nagging feeling that
something was missing. I could never define this feeling
exactly; it was simply a vague unrest, an impression that
life was passing by at second best: in Maeterlinck's phrase
'a nameless, hopeless distress'. Surely this was not all?
There must be something else, some deeper experience,
something at any rate to give a meaning to this banal
succession of days. By the time I reached my university I
decided that travel was the answer; that was the missing
thing. I must see for myself at first hand the places and the
peoples I had been reading about and hearing about all my
life. The Trip began to assume enormous importance in
my mind; the Trip to England first, of course, and then
anywhere so long as it was motion in a new direction. I
used to go down to the docks at Port Melbourne and read
on the sterns of the vessels the names of the wonderful
places from which they had sailed. Valparaiso. Liverpool.
San Francisco. Le Havre. Tokyo. One day, I said to myself. One day I will set off.

When eventually I did embark it was rather a mundane
affair. It was a comfortable one-class tourist ship, the
Ormonde, bound for Tilbury, and I travelled with friends I
had known for years. This was the great adventure, but
somehow it was swallowed up in the sane, comfortable,
reassuring sort of things I had been doing all my life;
tennis on the boat-deck, change for dinner, and then
dancing the foxtrot and the charleston to the ship's

orchestra. We played cards, there were little drinking parties in one another's cabins, and in no time at all we knew everyone on board remarkably well. There were the Simpson girls from Adelaide. The Brown family who used to live in the same street in Ballarat. Old Jack or Geoff with whom I had attended tutorials at the university; and so on. We made up jolly parties and went ashore at each of the ports, and I enjoyed it all immensely. And yet where was the answer to the mystery, the thing that was going to be revealed to me now that at last I had got away?

We sailed across the Indian Ocean to Colombo (a bathe at Lavinia Beach and dinner at the Galleface Hotel), across the Arabian Sea to the Canal and Port Said (shopping in the bazaar), through the Mediterranean to Naples (visit to Pompeii and Vesuvius) and then, one bright June morning in 1936, we steamed into Toulon harbour.

I date my life from this moment. Everything in my memory either falls into the period before I reached Toulon, or belongs to the years since then, and in fact my life abruptly took a new course that morning.

It was high tide—rather an exaggerated high tide for the Mediterranean—and the water in the harbour came up to within an inch or two of the stone coping on the docks. The waterfront of Toulon has been destroyed and rebuilt since then, and I do not think it can ever again be quite so lovely as it was. From the distance it had the effect of a mirage, some turreted town from the East, floating on the edge of the water. We anchored a good way out in the harbour and came ashore in small boats; and once ashore the city swallowed you up.

You stepped from your boat straight on to the cobblestones, and all about you yelling women were selling oysters and mussels, lobsters and crabs, shrimps and limpets and sea urchins; they were all alive, reeking of the sea, and piled on top of one another in sagging wicker baskets. Beyond these stalls there was a short open space and then the cafés began, dozens of rickety little tables in the sunshine, with coloured sunshades, and sitting there, idly surveying the universe, sipping their vermouth-cassis, were the bottomlessly cynical French clientele. Wonderfully gay little men, chattering like monkeys. And girls. French girls, doing things or having things done to them, right there in the open in a way that would have caused a riot back in Park Villas, Melbourne. Before my eyes a man casually reached up his hand to the waitress, pulled down her head, and kissed her on the mouth. When, after a long time, she lifted up her head again and caught my eye she smiled pleasantly. And in the corner, propped against a barrel of oysters, a woman opened the black front of her dress, pulled out her breast, and began to feed a baby. I imagine all the rest of the customers were behaving in a perfectly normal way, but these two incidents chanced to take place just at that moment and they hit my eye with a cyclonic shock. The shock no doubt was all the greater because this was precisely the sort of behaviour that I expected from the French—expected but never quite dared to believe was true. It was like having one's secret thoughts dragged out into the open, shamelessly and almost brutally. I shifted my eyes away uneasily. Beyond the cafés the façade of topsy-turvy buildings rose up, and they were painted in the brightest possible pale blues and yellows, with window boxes and strings of corn-cobs hanging out from the balconies to dry. It was a little reminiscent, I thought, of the last scene in Miss Moncrieff's *Maid of the Mountains*. But this was real, and the noise was stupendous. Everyone seemed to be shouting and in an incomprehensible gabble of words.

I left my friends then and walked on alone trying with my schoolboy French to decipher the advertisements and the slogans on the walls. Finally I came to an open square, a long oblong space flanked on each side by tall buildings and with an avenue of plane trees in full leaf running down the centre. This was the crisis for me. As I stood there on the sidewalk I knew that I would never go home again— not at any rate for many years.

It was market morning. The fishermen and the peasants had set up their stalls under the plane trees. There it was, the ripeness of the Midi, the colour, the shouting, and the confusion. Vast piles of cherries, peaches, and apricots. Wagon-loads of young carrots. Algerian bananas hanging on the branch, and cheeses like cartwheels. Nuts and strawberries and banks of flowers. On one side the butchers, on the other the clothing stalls, the wine-sellers and the pastrycooks. A small boy was using the bole of a plane tree as a public lavatory, half a dozen mongrels were running after a bitch, and somewhere in the distance under the interlacing shade and sunshine a concertina was playing. Everyone was buying or selling, trotting up and down, arguing fiercely and gesticulating; and a little group of sailors with red pompoms on their heads leaned against an advertisement for a bullfight which, as far as I could make out, had taken place a week before. A news-vendor was shouting hoarsely: ' *Crise financielle.*'

I walked slowly up the square between the stalls. This was it. This was what I had come for. Here in this market and among these people was the missing thing. From now on there was no more time to be lost: I must learn this language, I must understand what they were saying and thinking; and I must see all the other markets, the buildings, the paintings, and the peoples of Europe.

It is, of course, all too easy to aggrandize an emotion, and especially so pleasant an emotion as this, and after so long a time. But I do not think that I was only captivated by the gaiety and delightful strangeness of Toulon that morning. It was more of a feeling of recognition. I really did recognize each aspect of the scene—the music of the concertina, the shape of the wine glasses, the gesture made by the butcher's hand. Or at any rate these things seemed familiar to me and I walked about with entire confidence as though I had been here many times before. None of my ancestors were French or even from the Continent—they all came from Scotland and England—and it is too much to think that there was some kind of inherited memory here; that some predecessor of mine had lived on the Mediterranean, and that through three generations in Australia these scenes had been transmitted in some mysterious way to my mind. Yet the affinity was there. In my blood there was something that made me respond immediately and as spontaneously as a diviner's rod bends to water. And I knew then that my nostalgia had evaporated. I had come home. This was where I wanted to be.

It was ten years before I went back to Australia, and after that another six years went by before I returned on another visit. I myself must certainly have changed in all this time but I believe that Australia, or rather the contemporaries I left behind there, have changed even more. They are no longer an appendage of Europe; they are emerging into something quite different.

Somewhere in his *Journals* André Gide says that America has no soul because she has not yet 'deigned to plunge into the abyss of suffering and sin' (this was written before the First World War), and elsewhere he makes the point that a man can only find himself through suffering. Bernard Berenson added to this one day when I was with him. He said he believed that no people ever felt secure until they had begun to persecute someone else. Thus, the Pilgrim Fathers found their strength and their identity in the struggle against the Red Indians in America. And thus presumably the Spaniards against the natives in South America, the Jews against the Arabs in Israel, and so on, with all countries everywhere.

Australia in the nineteen-fifties would seem to me to lie somewhere between these two ideas. When I lived there as a boy and a young man she had not suffered very greatly.

The Boer War was not much more than an expedition, and although the First World War destroyed an incredibly large number of Australians it was war at a distance; at no time was Australia herself directly threatened. The soldiers left their wives and children secure in their homes behind them. But in the last war Australians really did suffer, both psychologically and physically. They suffered a defeat in Singapore, and when the Japanese came on and bombed Darwin and even shelled Sydney Harbour, they knew for the first time the meaning of fear in their own homes. It had one immediate result; as soon as the war was over Australia began to welcome migrants into the country in a way which would have been unthinkable twenty years ago. Scandinavians, Germans, Italians, and Poles as well as British have been pouring into the country in hundreds of thousands in the last five years. The original British stock may eventually become submerged, but no matter; anything to fill up the empty spaces before another wave of Asiatics breaks upon them in another war.

Australia has not yet advanced to the second stage; she does not yet feel secure and she has not yet begun to persecute anybody (we can scarcely count the aborigines, they were too few and too helpless). She knows that for the next decade at least she will be dependent in another crisis upon outside help, probably from America.

All these things are weakening the ties with Europe, and especially England. Instead, a new independence grows up steadily, year by year, and with this independence the new traditions which are peculiarly Australian. It was the stage through which America must have passed soon after the Civil War when she began erecting her own legends and heroes, Jefferson and Washington, the cults of the South and the West, and the conscious power of big machines and big business. There is still no history inside Australia, or at any rate no history in the terms of civil wars, or the renaissance of the arts, or of any past civiliza-

tion which has risen and decayed. But already the cattleman and the sheepman in the bush are people in their own
right, living a life which knows very little of the outside
world, and their children look back, not to England, but
to the story of their own Australian ancestors. And in the
cities the descendants of the big business and mining
families take on a colour which is peculiarly their own. It
is said there is a deficiency in the soil in Australia, an
absence of salts or some other lack in the water. After
two or three generations livestock begins to decline, and
the blood has to be renewed by importing thoroughbreds
from England and France. No one has dared to suggest
that this applies to human beings, but it is certainly true
of racehorses and perhaps poultry, pigs, dogs, and a number of other creatures as well. The one notable exception
is the Merino sheep, which was originally brought from
North Africa and now flourishes on the dry hot plains of
the Australian riverina rather better than anywhere else
in the world.

But presumably beasts like human beings will adjust
themselves to anything in the long run, and eventually a
whole range of new species will be developed here, as
strange and indigenous as the koala bear and the kangaroo.

For expatriates like me there are, of course, regrets. We
find ourselves increasingly out of date and trapped in a
new nostalgia for the days when everything was an experi-
ment and a discovery, and there was always lurking in the
background the comfortable reassurance of the traditions
of England.

When we go back to Australia now we do not admire
the roaring streets of Sydney, a city of two millions, one
of the largest in the world, for it seems to us to be an
imitation of another kind, Chicago perhaps. The strip
lighting, the advertisements, and the movies—these are
the things from which we are trying to escape; and we
liked Sydney Harbour much better before the famous

bridge was built. It used to be great fun coming across to Circular Quay in a ferry boat. All this new part of Australia of which the Australians are understandably proud—the great dockyards and the department stores—you can see anywhere from Liverpool to Kansas City and São Paulo in Brazil.

So we creep off to the bush, the old indestructible. We peer at the kangaroos and the native corroborees with delight and astonishment. They are all doomed, no doubt, and they hang on a little incongruously in a world where there is really no place for them and no certain future. The future belongs to atomic power and the uranium mine at Rum Jungle.

The chapters that follow here are largely the result of my last trip to Australia, when I travelled through the centre and the northern part of the country, the part that is mainly uninhabited. All this area was as strange to me as the jungles of Borneo and the African deserts. As a boy I had simply heard about it and passionately hoped that one day I would be able to go there. So in a sense this was a journey back into my childhood, the fulfilment of an old wish: it really belongs to that half of my life which came to an end so unexpectedly on that bright June morning in the harbour of Toulon.

CHAPTER TWO

Stuart and the Ghan

THE Northern Territory is a big country, about one-third the size of Europe, with a couple of sizeable deserts in the centre. But all the rest is good grazing land and a queer kind of jungle where mangrove swamps, eucalyptus scrub, kangaroos, crocodiles, and even tree pythons are mixed up together in a way that does not occur anywhere else.

Gold has been picked up close to the surface in remarkable quantities, and hardly a year goes by without someone emerging from the north with stories of rich finds in silver, lead, zinc, tin, and half a dozen other minerals. Latterly the big cattle stations (they range from the size of an English county upward) have been making money to the tune of hundreds of thousands of pounds every year. During the war, when the Australian and American armies moved in for a brief space to meet an expected Japanese invasion, some of the troops tried their hand at market gardening, and they found that in no time at all they were producing mammoth watermelons, cabbages, and tomatoes, in fact almost anything they cared to put into the ground from pineapples to tobacco and coffee seemed to leap up in a tropical frenzy.

And yet there is a hoodoo on the place. Somehow, for one reason or another, people tend to give up after a year or two and drift away to the south again. At the last census there were less than 30,000 inhabitants in the Northern Territory; and that included the aborigines and the half-castes as well as the whites.

It was a Scot named John McDouall Stuart who first

started the Eldorado legend. He came out to Australia from Edinburgh in 1838, a keen young blade of twenty-one in a billycock hat and stovepipe trousers; and there appears to have been nothing really exceptional about him except his utter determination. Those were the days when Europe was six months away by sailing ship and all Australia was wide open. There was a passion to discover what lay in the centre of the continent (one has to remember that it is just about the same size as the United States), and before long the South Australian government was offering a reward to the first man who made the two-thousand-mile journey from Adelaide in the south to the Indian Ocean in the tropical north.

Stuart decided he was the man for the job. Mounted on his little bay mare Polly, carrying only flour and dried meat as provisions, he made six separate attempts to break across the unexplored country. Each journey took him from six months to a year and each time he got a little further. There were periods when he went blind and almost died through scurvy and starvation, but he kept going. His dour, uncompromising journals make strange reading now when so few men have their faith so absolutely fixed or so slow an appreciation of the arts of publicity.

It was on the fourth journey that he arrived at the exact centre of Australia, a thousand miles from the sea. There he and his companions solemnly raised the British flag on a mountain top. 'We then', says Stuart, 'gave three hearty cheers for the flag, the emblem of civil and religious liberty, and may it be a sign to the natives that the dawn of liberty, civilization, and Christianity is about to break on them.'

The natives, however, were not quite ready for the dawn of liberty. In full war-paint they closed in on Stuart and his party, and with a fearful yell sent their boomerangs whistling round his ears. Stuart got away under the cover of darkness and beat a retreat to Adelaide.

His sixth and final attempt to cross the continent was made with twelve men and forty-nine horses; and it did not start very auspiciously. Some of his horses collapsed through thirst and exhaustion, and one of his men deserted. Nor were the naked natives much more friendly; to them, a white man mounted on a horse was some monstrous apparition from the ancestral past, and certainly evil. Stuart records that on 5 March 1862, his party came up to a waterhole where a black and his lubra (the native word for wife) were fishing. 'The female was the first who left the water; she ran to the bank, took up her child, and made for a tree, up which she climbed, pushing her young one up before her. She was a tall, well-made woman. The man (an old fellow), tall, stout, and robust, although startled at our appearance, took it leisurely in getting out of the water, ascended the bank, and had a look at us; he then addressed us in his own language, and seemed to work himself up into a great passion, stopping every now and then and spitting fiercely at us like an old tiger. He also ascended the tree and then gave us a second edition of it.'

Stuart watered his horses under the old man's curses and passed on. It was a long and dreary journey but he had at least the joys that only explorers know; the sight of 'a new kind of Macaw', flocks of brilliant cockatoos and parrots, new kinds of kangaroos, lizards, trees and flowers, which no white man had ever seen before. And he had a splendid time naming each new mountain range and river after his friends and sponsors back in Adelaide. Just occasionally the party got a wallaby or a wild goose to add to their rations.

On Thursday, 24 July 1862, eight months out from his base, Stuart found by his compass bearing that he was on the point of reaching the sea. He said nothing to the rear-guard of his party, but pushed his way on foot through the thick scrub on to the beach and, he says, 'was delighted to behold the water of the Indian Ocean in Van Diemen's Gulf, before the party with the horses knew anything of its proximity. Thring, who rode in advance of me, called out "The Sea!" which so took them all by surprise, and they were so astonished, that he had to repeat the call before they fully understood what was meant.'

Stuart dipped his feet and washed his hands and face in the water. There followed a ceremony which echoes a little sadly across to the twentieth century, and which was as odd as any native rite in that lonely and outlandish place. The party, now half starved and in rags, gathered together on the beach. A tall tree close to the sea was stripped of its branches, and the Union Jack with Stuart's name sewn in the centre of it was fixed to the top. 'When this was completed, the party gave three cheers, and Mr. Kekwick [Stuart's second in command] then addressed me, congratulating me on having completed this great and important undertaking, to which I replied. Mr. Waterhouse [the expedition's naturalist] also spoke a few words on the same subject, and concluded with three cheers for the Queen and three for the Prince of Wales.' They then buried at the foot of the tree a note in an airtight container saying who they were and what they had done.

In his journal on this day something of Stuart's exuberance breaks through his steady prose. 'I feel confident', he wrote, 'that if a new settlement is formed in this splendid country, in a few years it will become one of the brightest gems of the British crown.' The soil, he reported, was 'of the richest nature ever formed for the benefit of mankind'. The country was abundantly supplied with fresh water. There was every kind of timber from the casurina to bamboo, sixty feet high. The rivers abounded in fish and waterfowl of every description. There were even signs of gold and other minerals. All that remained to be done was to populate the place and bring to the natives the benefits and enlightenment of civilization.

The four months' journey back to Adelaide was a dreadful business. Stuart, half blind and maddened with stomach troubles, 'a sad, sad wreck of former days', was so weak he had to be carried some of the way on a stretcher between two horses. Twelve months and thirteen days after he first set out he rode into the city to receive the government reward of £2,000, a gold medal, and a watch from the Royal Geographical Society. He returned to London and a year or two later he was dead, unmarried, at the age of forty-eight. However, he lived just long enough to see his journals published, and with that the Eldorado legend and the turgid history of the north began.

Nobody yet has quite succeeded in straightening out the story of the early pioneers who followed Stuart's route up into the unknown. There were gold and silver rushes, land booms, and cotton booms. The first of the cattle kings came up from the south driving their beasts for a year along the track until they found new grasslands which they simply seized and made their own; and the cattle rustlers—known as 'poddy dodgers'—followed close behind. There were crazy expeditions after buffalo and crocodiles, and every year or so in London and Melbourne there would be a sudden wave of hysterical investment of the kind that dates back to the South Sea Bubble. A man had only to turn up in the big cities in the south with a pocketful of black opals or a bag of pearls and it was enough for another rush to start towards the north.

Often the men who set out on the two-thousand-mile journey had no more knowledge of the bush than you can pick up in the bar of a city pub; and before long quite a few of them died of thirst or exhaustion, or simply vanished. Many of those who straggled back to civilization were gaunt with hunger and burnt to a dark brown by the sun, but they had one thing in common: they were determined to try again.

The next fifty years are a story of hardship that grows

monotonous by repetition. The cattle were either speared by the natives or demolished by a venomous tick brought in by accident from the East Indies. Riots broke out in the mining camps, when the whites either fought among themselves or tried to oust the Malays and the Chinese who had come in by sampan across the Timor Sea. Floods and droughts seem to have succeeded one another in a rhythm as regular as the tides, and when Vesteys, the English firm, invested a million pounds in building a meat works in the far north it was only a matter of a few years before the enterprise collapsed.

By the time the last war arrived it seemed only natural that the Japanese should pick on Darwin, the capital of the Northern Territory, for their most drastic air raids, and they almost succeeded in demolishing the town.

A few families have managed to survive these disasters, and they, together with the government officials and the natives, make up the bulk of the 30,000 who inhabit the Northern Territory now. But the Stuart legend dies hard. Many of these people still believe that they are living in the midst of an Eldorado, and that the colony will indeed become one of the brightest gems of the Crown one day. And as though to confirm them in their faith something quite new has recently arrived on the scene. Late in 1949 a prospector named Jack White turned up in Darwin with a collection of grey rocks, which he said he had picked up at a place named Rum Jungle some fifty miles to the south. On examination these rocks were found to contain more than two per cent of uranium, which is a very good proportion indeed.

The extent of the field has not yet been determined, but there is already enough evidence to show that Rum Jungle may be at least equal in importance to the Congo and the Canadian fields—and the chances are that it will become the richest single uranium mine in the world. And since things rarely happen in isolation, three other discoveries

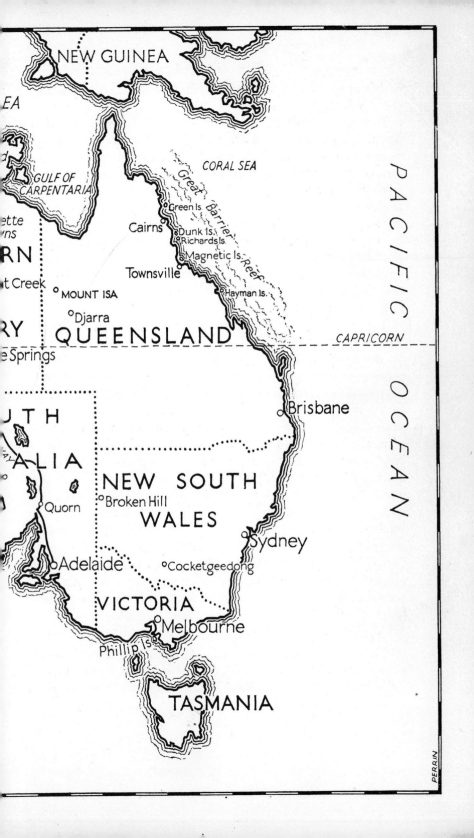

in bauxite, silver-lead-zinc and tin have come to light in the north at the same time.

Not unnaturally, in these circumstances, the Eldorado dream has got away to a promising new start, as promising as anything envisaged by John McDouall Stuart; and in a strange way Stuart and his faith still dominate the situation. When you go north from Adelaide now you follow precisely upon his route, seeing the places he saw and named, and in the end feeling pretty much the same way as he did. It is not the twentieth-century improvements that strike you; it is the absence of them, the sense you have that time has been standing still here, that the isolation is permanent, and that the real future of the country still lies somewhere over the horizon.

There is a narrow-gauge railway now that runs up from Adelaide for a thousand miles to the town of Alice Springs on the tropic of Capricorn, just south of the centre of the continent. Most people with cars tend to drive the first couple of hundred miles to a place called Quorn, and there they put their cars on the train, since there is nothing but a semi-desert track for the next eight hundred miles. That train is still something of an oddity in the world. It runs once a week and it is divided into two parts. The front section is called the Afghan, or more briefly the Ghan—a name that has descended from the early days when camels were the chief method of transport and camel-drivers, imported from Aghanistan, were the most regular passengers on the line. The back section of the train, the one that carries the cars on open flat-top trucks, goes by the pleasant name of the Chaser. For two days and nights the Ghan and the Chaser bowl across the plains, almost the only sign of life in that endless space.[1]

On Quorn station a printed time-table is displayed, but

[1] There is a rival and perhaps more plausible theory that the Ghan got its name from the native word for smoke; but there seems to be little hope now of disentangling the real origin of the word.

there is no pedantry about this. The sunshine streams
down, the hours pass, and when the passengers in the
waiting-room grow a little restive the station master
reassures them: 'She'll be along. She's due in all right this
afternoon.'

Equally it is difficult to get advance information about
when you are likely to arrive at Alice Springs. The Ghan
and the Chaser are regulated not by hours or minutes but
by days. 'She'll be there Saturday,' the station master says.
'Saturday or Sunday.'

However, the train *does* get into Quorn eventually,
some time in the evening on Thursdays; sheep, goats,
cars, machinery, crates of beer, and passengers are loaded
on board in a slow confusion, and away you go into the
darkness of the desert. Since this is no ordinary train
journey—it more resembles a voyage on a ship—the passengers are not of the ordinary kind, and they tend to
strike up rapid friendships. It would be a dull trip on the
Ghan if you did not meet (as I did) a fairly wide cross-
section of humanity, including a group of Jehovah Wit-
nesses, a water-diviner, three nuns, a liquor salesman, a
party of buffalo shooters, and a man who in his early days
had been a promising amateur balloonist.

Those who have berths on the train sleep two in a compartment, one above the other; and since you are bound to
spend at least the next forty-eight hours in close intimacy
it is important to have a congenial travelling companion.
On the whole I was lucky. My man was a muscular young
fellow, dark, and very good-looking. He sat on the edge
of his bunk, nodding and smiling agreeably, but never
actually speaking. For some time we gazed out at the
bright desert stars—they seem to be twice the size in that
clear air, and the Southern Cross is as sharply defined as
an electric sign on a hilltop—and I began to realize that
he could not speak a word of English. Obviously he was
one of the European emigrants who have been arriving

Information Service Australia House, London

Alice Springs

in Australia in such numbers since the end of the war.

Looking at his dark curly hair I asked, 'Are you an Italian?'

'No,' he said in Italian, 'I was born in Italy but I am an Australian.'

'Well,' I said heartily, 'it's a funny thing: I was born in Australia and now I live in Italy.'

He did not appear to be greatly moved by this information; on the contrary, he developed a slightly defensive attitude. He was even reluctant to speak in Italian, and began lapsing back into a kind of sign language whenever he could.

'It must be difficult in Australia when you first arrive,' I said.

'I haven't just arrived,' he said. 'I've been here eighteen months.'

'And yet you speak no English?'

'There's no need. I meet Italians wherever I go.'

'But now,' I said. 'You're going to a little place—Alice Springs. You won't find any Italians there.'

'Yes I will,' he said. 'I've had a job there before.'

He had had, in fact, nine separate jobs in Australia since the previous year, sometimes in the cities and sometimes in the remotest possible places in the bush. In the course of the next two days I learned a good deal about emigrants (known locally as New Australians), and more particularly about the new life of my friend Bruno.

I happen to know the village where he was born, and in a country like Italy, where there are permanently two million unemployed, it is the kind of place where the poverty bites deepest. In that village there are often earthen floors in the houses, and ten or a dozen in the family with little or no work for any of them. Now, here was Bruno in a country where many thousands of jobs are advertised in the newspapers every week, and at wages which the entire family could never have dreamed of back in Italy. He was moving about, travelling first class on the trains, taking up jobs just so long as they amused him, and then moving on again. He lit a cigarette, opened up a bottle of grappa and handed it to me. He did not want to be reminded of Italy. The side of *bella Italia* he had known had been a washout; now he was an Australian. As soon as this was understood between us we got on very well, and we bowled along Stuart's route to the north talking eagerly about gold, cattle, uranium, and racehorses with the amateur balloonist and the liquor salesman.

Beer, the national drink of Australia, is consumed in that dry atmosphere of the interior at a pace which is a gastronomical phenomenon. Along the whole of that thousand miles from Adelaide to Alice Springs there is one unbroken line of empty bottles which have been hurled out of the train by a generation of passengers. Every few hours the Ghan halts at some wayside station to replenish supplies. That is the moment when the passengers swarm from the train into the bright clear sunshine and make directly for the pub, a little corrugated iron shack that stands beside the track. There, standing at the counter, they drink until the engine-driver feels it is time to move on again. He gives a first blast on his whistle as a warning, and then a second to indicate that he is definitely getting under way. Then the passengers, bottle in hand, come coursing across the sand and leap aboard the step of the moving train.

All this area to the north of South Australia has a very low rainfall indeed, and to an eye accustomed to the broken outlines and the rapid movement of the city there is, at first, very little to see. The flat monotonous plains stretch away until they lose themselves in a watery mirage on the horizon. But then, little by little, the traveller sheds his sense of urgency; after a day of this gently rocking motion (the Ghan seldom moves faster than twenty-five miles an hour), he begins to feel that he might have been sitting here for ever, suspended in time and space, and the beginning and the ending of the journey cease to have much importance. This is the point—it occurred with me just at dusk on the second day—when some sort of adjustment takes place in your brain and you begin to see with new eyes. It's rather like putting on a pair of those spectroscopic spectacles which give a third dimension to a photograph and make each object stand out in perspective. A single tree in the distance becomes an event. It stands up in isolation; you see all round it, as it were, and you begin to know it as you would never know a tree in a forest. With human beings and the animals and birds the effect is redoubled, partly because they are so odd in themselves, but mainly because there are so few of them.

Bruno and I gazed entranced for a long time out of the window while two splendid black emus paced beside the train, nothing but a dry salt lake behind them. They put their great horny feet down on the sand and ran like monstrous chickens, too addled in their bird-brains to know that by running beside the train they were not getting away from it. They stopped at last when the Ghan, with a major effort, began to overtake them, and they stood looking after us with shocked and indignant eyes. Those two birds are fixed in my mind more firmly than any emu I ever saw in a zoo. Occasionally, too, a kangaroo came bounding across the track, and one saw him, fore and aft, high in the air and thudding down on the ground for an instant until his fat tail propelled him into the sky again. Then he would stop, in an upright position, beneath a scraggy clump of spinifex, and put his two neat front paws together with a gentle little motion, almost in an attitude of prayer, while he watched us go by. When you have seen a kangaroo like that you really know what one looks like.

You come on the aborigines—or rather what the white men have made of the aborigines—directly you get into this country. If Stuart brought them the dawn of liberty

this surely must be the late afternoon. The men wear the
clothes of the Australian cattleman, which are not unlike
the Texan get-up, but with exotic flourishes. The hat is
round and flat on top, with a very wide brim, a little
reminiscent of a Spanish matador. His shirt, imported no
doubt by some enterprising salesman from the south,
tends to bright emerald greens and scarlets, with a scarf
knotted round the neck for use over the eyes and when dust
is blowing. His long spindly legs are encased in tight
pants which taper away into the strangest sort of boots, a
heritage from the gentlest traditions of Victorian England.
They are very thin-soled and they have elastic sides; the
sort of comfortable house-boot which Mr. Barrett of Wim-
pole Street might have slipped into when he got into his
smoking-cap and his padded jacket in the evening. The
virtue here, apparently, is that if a man slips from the
saddle and his foot catches in the stirrup, the boot will come
off and allow him to fall unhurt to the ground.

Underneath these trappings—and they tend to be very
torn and shoddy—the aborigine is an amiable fellow, with
a deeply sculptured face and very white teeth. A century
of tobacco, clothes, and white man's laws have not quite,
as yet, subdued a certain childish, feckless gaiety. His wife
with her bare feet, her print dress, and her child riding
sideways across her hip, is not quite so grand, but she
smiles too; and that helps to take the curse off the squalid
iron shed in which she lives, beside the railroad track.

All the rest of the scenery, once you get used to it, is
very fine indeed, provided that you like space, and it grows
finer still as the Ghan approaches Alice Springs. The rainfall is more plentiful in the centre (ten inches a year), and
so the birds and animals increase, the semi-desert gradually
merges into a country of mulga scrub, clumps of tall
grasses, and occasional eucalyptus trees with snow-white
bark on their trunks; in this country trees keep their
leaves through the winter but shed their bark. Little by

little the plains break up into low ridges (known as 'go-downs'), and the sand-dunes are so deeply impregnated with iron that they glow blood-red, especially in the evening light.

Since the Ghan is almost the only regular connection with the outside world, its once-weekly arrival is an event in Alice Springs. We got in more or less on time just as it was approaching dusk on Saturday night, and were accorded the same honours as a cargo steamer arriving at some remote island in the ocean. Long before we sighted the town half a dozen cars and a batch of cattlemen on motor-cycles came out to meet us. They ran alongside dodging through the gum trees and calling out to their friends on board. We carried the beer and the mail and we were welcome. Then the Ghan gave one final triumphant blast on its whistle, plunged through a gap in the Mac-donnell ranges, and drew up panting at the station.

CHAPTER THREE

The Alice

FOR some reason the general hoodoo on the north has never touched Alice Springs, and it is like no other place in Australia. Perhaps it's the remoteness—it is roughly a thousand miles from any other town—and the height above sea-level (nearly 2,000 feet), which gives it a winter climate like Morocco or Arizona: cold nights and bright yellow sunshine through the day. The Todd river that runs through the town is hardly a river at all, but then you can dig down twelve feet anywhere about the town and come on good clear water.

Nearly all the bush towns of the north are cursed with the lack of women, which has the effect of driving the men to the bookies and the pubs for their recreation, but there seems to be a superabundance of pretty girls in Alice Springs. In midwinter you see them in dozens in their summer dresses moving down a line of bright shops and cafés on the main street.

These things have created a curious sort of buoyancy in the town, and you can't stay there for half an hour before you begin to feel it. After a week you find yourself contemplating the idea of settling down for good. To the local people (there are only 4,000 of them), and the men who ride in from the cattle stations and the mines round about, Alice Springs is always 'The Alice'. It is not so much a town as a pleasant idea, having a special flavour of its own like The Hague in Holland. The gender of the idea is feminine, and in fact the place is named after a certain Alice Todd whose husband built the overland telegraph line from Adelaide to Darwin.

I went one evening to play lawn tennis at a homestead
on the outskirts of the town. There was a swimming-pool
in the garden, and beyond that, through the tamarisks
and the orange groves, a stretch of desert leading up to
the bare Macdonnell ranges that make a ring round the
valley. These hills create a false sunset that runs on for
forty minutes or more since they block the direct rays of
the sun, though the sun itself is still above the horizon.
By some trick of refraction the light then pours down on
you from the empty sky above, and from the east; and this
moment is the more remarkable because the rocks in the
hills, which are brick-red by day, slowly begin to glow in
shades of yellow and scarlet, and finally resolve themselves into solid lumps of greenish-purple and dark indigo,
and the atmosphere is completely still. Even the white
tennis balls have a splash of colour on them as they fly
through the air.

Everything in The Alice is touched in some way by this
hectic light. The people like to show you their opals, the
most valuable stones in the territory. They spread them
out over the rugs on the floor, and in the black opals
especially you see the same clear colours of the sunset, a
kind of miniature of the surrounding sky, and almost as
luminous. I was looking at some of these stones when a
boy came in and asked if I was interested in birds as well.
Presently he came back with a covey of them fluttering
about his head. I had seen the flocks of greyish-pink and
white galahs, the laughing jackasses, and the sulphur-
crested cockatoos that were constantly flying overhead;
but these were rarer varieties, notably a greenish-blue bird
with a slightly phosphorescent light in his feathers, and
Major Mitchell cockatoos that screamed and lifted up
bright scarlet crests when they were disturbed. They were
tame but jealous. When two of the Major Mitchells
lighted on my shoulder I was fiercely attacked by an outsize pigeon with a murderous beak. Then the room was

filled with beating wings and unbearable screechings, rather like a Technicolor film when the sound track goes wrong, or an early attempt at colour television.

At the tennis party there was a girl of exceptional beauty, even by the standards of Alice Springs. She was very grave and direct in a pleasant way. When we were sitting in the garden watching the light in the sky she said to me, 'I will never leave this place. This is where I want to be.' She said she used to ride out alone each day into the bare hills, for an hour or two, just to see the rocks and the ghost gums round the waterholes. There was indeed a kind of Wordsworthian devotion in the way she spoke about the country, and although she looked more like a film star than a girl from the outback (she had very long bare legs and shorts that must have been bought in some sophisticated city store), she was obviously sincere, if incoherent. 'I don't know,' she kept saying, 'I can't explain.'

I asked what had brought her to The Alice in the first place, and she answered, with a slight air of anticlimax, 'The movies'. Six years before, she explained, she had been discovered in Sydney by the movie people, and under the name of Daphne Campbell had been given the leading part in a film about the Australian cattle country called *The Overlanders*. A good deal of the film had been shot in the Northern Territory, and it was a success. After the British and American premieres, telegrams began to arrive for Miss Campbell offering contracts in Hollywood and London; but by that time she had seen Alice Springs. She married a pilot in one of the airlines that run between the outback stations, and except for one or two holidays visits to the cities in the south had never since left the centre of Australia.

She turned up next day in a torn pair of jodhpurs and we went out to a place called Simpson's Gap, where the hills suddenly split into two sharp precipices, a faintly eerie

spot. There are a number of such places in the centre. The
most famous of them is Ayer's Rock, a huge pavilion of
stone, almost a mountain, that rises sheer out of the desert
without a living thing on it. Ayer's Rock lies hundreds of
miles away from the nearest homestead, in a waterless
plain, and white people are not supposed to go there since
the aborigines occasionally use it for their ceremonies.
Some of the caves which have recently been explored are
decorated with wall paintings and drawings: crude human
figures, kangaroos, lizards, and a repeated series of abstract
designs which apparently have some tribal meaning, and
are certainly related to sex. The floor of at least one dark
cave is matted with blood from circumcision rituals which
have gone on since time beyond history. Simpson's Gap is
less spectacular, but it has the feeling of the blackfellows
about it, the sense of oldness and antediluvian time that
pervades everything in the Australian bush. The land
itself looks worn down and tired (it is, indeed, one of the
oldest geological continents), and even the leaves of the
eucalypts hang downwards a little wearily. The empty beer
bottles left by the last tourists and the bright birds rushing through the branches don't quite succeed in dragging
you back to the present again. Miss Campbell stood on an
obsidian green rock and looked up at a vermilion cliff
where two eagles were circling about lazily. 'You see,'
she said, 'I love this place but I can't explain it.'

In Alice Springs occasionally you will see a three-ton
truck being driven through the town. Painted boldly on
the sides are the words 'Albert Namatjira, Artist'. At the
wheel, surrounded by his relatives and friends, is Albert
himself, a solid, comfortable-looking aborigine; and it is
probably true to say that he has done more to describe the
centre of Australia than any other single man. Albert is a
member of the Aranda tribe living at the Hermansburg
Mission about a hundred miles to the west of Alice Springs.
It is some years ago now that Rex Battarbee, a white

artist, was painting there and got to know the natives fairly well. Albert especially showed a passionate interest in Battarbee's work, and when he said one day, 'I think I could do that myself', Battarbee handed him a brush, a piece of paper, and some water-colours. Albert got to work and has never stopped since.

Most aborigines approach painting with the same direct and uninhibited methods that children do; if a thing catches their eye they put it in, the brighter and bolder the better, a technique which, though fresh, is a little weak on perspective and design. But from the first Albert showed remarkable powers. He imitated Battarbee, and then having got the hang of the thing began to launch out for himself with an aboriginal's hypersensitive feeling for the bush where he was born. His birds and animals were nicely observed (he noted, for instance, that at a waterhole one emu will keep watch for enemies while his mate stoops to drink); but he found his real vocation in straight landscape. The mad range of purples and oranges in the Hermansburg hills were as natural to Albert as the air he breathed, and he got them down on paper with great fidelity. When Battarbee began to exhibit these early efforts in public, there was an instant reaction. City Australians tend to regard aborigines as little more than cretins. But here was one of them who actually painted, and such odd and pretty landscapes too. They began by buying Albert's paintings as they would buy a boomerang or any other souvenir, and they ended by buying them as works of art and an investment. A boom began down in the art galleries of Adelaide, Sydney, and Melbourne. Today Albert's paintings bring fifty guineas upward, and he is one of the best known and most highly paid artists in Australia.

The effect of all this on the Aranda tribe has been disturbing. Among the aborigines all things are communal: if Albert could paint, why not everyone else? It was a nice restful occupation. Albert's sons and nephews set to work with gusto, and even some of his female relatives joined in. At Hermansburg Mission today there is a flourishing studio, and Battarbee is hard put to it to keep the flood of art under some sort of control. As the creator of this renaissance and the representative of the Australian Fine Arts Council he has the double-headed job of encouraging the good black artists and keeping the bad white dealers at bay. Albert Namatjira's work will sell anywhere any day of the week, while his nephews (known presumably as the Followers or the School of Namatjira) can only hope to raise a pound or two from the buyers. It was not long before the tribe discovered that the magic lay in the word 'Namatjira'; that was what the whites were paying for. So why not put the magic signature at the bottom of their own paintings and rake in fifty guineas a time? Mr. Battarbee had to explain patiently that this was not cricket. Nevertheless a few forgeries got through.

Nowadays in Alice Springs you can legally buy Aranda paintings only from Battarbee himself; he puts the Fine Arts stamp on them, vouches for their authenticity, and collects the money. Even the money has caused headaches, since the aborigines are still unused to handling it, and when they do get a roll of banknotes invariably lose it to the first unscrupulous white. Namatjira is given an allowance (out of which he bought his three-ton truck and now supports his relatives), and the rest is held in trust for him or devoted to furthering the work of the mission at Hermansburg.

There is one other institution they speak of with pride in Alice Springs, and that is the Flying Doctor Radio Service. Originally the idea was that there should always be a doctor on hand ready to fly off in an emergency to the outback stations—some of them hundreds of miles away from civilization. Each homestead was supplied with a radio and a call-sign, and for the first time in their lives the country people had a chance of getting medical atten-

tion within a few hours. But now the service goes much
further than this.

From the headquarters in the hospital at Alice Springs
regular transmissions go out five times a day. It is not
unlike a party line, but on a much larger scale, and since
the issues are either pretty desperate or of the absurd and
pathetic kind that reveal people's private lives, one listens
like an eavesdropper, with a mixture of fascination and
embarrassment. The service is run by a brisk young man
named Graham Pitts, and by now he has got the house-
wives fairly well trained in the technicalities of radio. He
opens up with a conversational 'good morning', and asks
first for the 'medicals'—anyone in the homesteads for a
thousand miles around who has urgent need of a doctor.
Half a dozen voices come in at once giving their call signs:
'Uncle William', 'Dog Apple', 'Henry Baker', and so on.

'All right,' Pitt says, 'I'll take Uncle William first.
Good morning, Mrs. Brady, what's the matter? Over.'

A wearied, rather frightened voice comes through. 'It's
our girl, Betty. We've been up all night with her. She
can't eat and she goes hot and cold and she's got a head-
ache; and I know you've got all that polio down at Alice.'
There is a pause, then: 'Oh, I forgot. Over.'

'Just a minute, Mrs. Brady. I'll put you through to the
doctor.'

The doctor, hooked up to the radio by phone, asks Mrs.
Brady a number of questions, tells her to give three pills
from the bottle marked No. 5 from her medicine chest (all
the stations have been given numbered bottles of drugs
and medicines), and to check back on the late afternoon
service.

Dog Apple, five hundred miles away in another direction, had a native stockman with a broken leg—a wild
steer had crushed him in the yards that morning—and the
doctor said he would fly out around midday. Would they
get someone to clear away the anthills from the home

paddock, he added; he had a lot of trouble landing his plane last time.

After the medicals Pitt announced that he had fifteen telegrams for various people, and forty minutes went by while he read them out and got the replies. One man, with an imperative note in his voice, wanted a bet on the two-thirty at Adelaide; someone else had a broken windmill and needed spare parts, quick; a third man on holiday down in Sydney had had a bit of bad luck which, he said, he would explain later, and meanwhile could the family send him fifty pounds? Another voice, a woman's, asked patiently if there was any news of her baby who had been flown into hospital yesterday, a suspected case of infantile paralysis (yes, Pitts said, it was polio but they were doing all they could); and another man, stranded out on the West Australian border, wanted to know why his people hadn't blank well picked him up at Murphy's Creek like they said they would—he had been there since Tuesday. Up in the far north two mobs of cattle were headed for the same waterhole where there was sufficient water for only one mob at a time. Pitts sorted that out by calling the nearest cattle station and asking them to ride out and head one mob in a different direction. He then gave out the weather report, supplied some brief advice on how to handle a grasshopper plague, reprimanded one of his clients for letting his radio batteries run down, and announced finally, with a slight beading of perspiration on his forehead, that he was signing off until the next transmission at 2 p.m.

It is the size of this area to the north of Alice Springs—you could put all France, Spain, and Italy into it—that baulks the mind at first. Some of the cattle stations are countries in their own right, huge, unfenced tracts of rolling plains where the cattle roam free throughout the year. Many of the owners and managers have never fully explored their own properties.

Since the war prosperity has hit these places with curious effects. There never was time in the old days, let alone enough money, to engage very seriously in the finesse of civilized living. The station homesteads, often spaced fifty or a hundred miles apart, in an empty wilderness, were simply collections of huts and outbuildings built of roughly sawn timber and corrugated iron. Here the owner or the manager and his family lived together with the stockmen, the jackaroos (young men learning the work), the rouseabouts (men of all trades), cooks, and the aborigines. They never saw a stranger, sometimes for weeks on end. The children were educated by correspondence courses or not at all. There was no music, few books, and seldom a game of any kind. Life was work and a long succession of days, each one precisely like the last. Men spent, as they still do, ten hours a day or more in the saddle, and some of them were out alone in the bush for a month at a time, living no better than the explorer Stuart did, on tea, dried meat, and a concoction of flour, water, and salt which is called damper, and which they made themselves. The main events of life were disasters: broken legs, bush fires, cattle plagues, and floods.

But for the last ten years it has been no uncommon thing for a station to earn upwards of a hundred thousand pounds a year, and there is very little income tax in the Northern Territory. Here was the money flowing in and absolutely nothing in the way of luxury goods to spend it on—the nearest . shops were a thousand miles away. Gradually the cattlemen and their wives came south to the big cities to see the sights, and do a little shopping. Some of them liked it so much they stayed in town and sent managers up to run their properties. Others went back to the Northern Territory with new ideas about gracious living, and the results have been uneven, almost startling. They bought deep freezes, outsize radios, washing-up machines, air-conditioning sets, and entire electrical plants

Information Service Australia House, London

"The line bunches, parts in the middle, then joins again and strings away across the plain." Cattle droving in the Northern Territory

to run all these fabulous gadgets. They bought Rolls Royces and aeroplanes. Some of them went in for antique silver and period furniture.

There were, however, still no means of rebuilding their remote houses, and the bush itself is unchangeable and eternal. So the new gadgets had to go into the old pioneering huts and sheds as they stood. Air-conditioning was sometimes installed in rooms that still had an earthen floor and a hole in the roof for the smoke of the kitchen fire to escape. Flies and mosquitoes perched on the Georgian silver, and lizards were apt to get under the lid of the new grand piano. These things of course have straightened themselves out with time, and very many of the homesteads now are modern and comfortable places, with green gardens that have been forced into life against the endless sun. But the ancient and empty bush still lies just outside these oases, and it stretches away into infinity. And still the Rolls Royce stands out in the cattle paddock with perhaps three or four other cars of lush design which have taken the owner's eye on his last visit to town.

This juxtaposition of the infinitely primitive and the infinitely new—the aboriginal riding in the Rolls and the kangaroo bounding under the wings of the landing plane—is, to the tourist's eye, half the fun of the North. A Ming vase looks wonderful on an upturned box in an iron shed.

But it is the bush itself that is the overmastering thing; it forces every living thing to conform, and the homesteads are nothing more than tiny islands in space. In this country everything is governed by water. Every journey is a journey towards water; every homestead stands where it does because there is water close by. Except in the far north, there are no permanent rivers, and only a few months of rainfall each year. The water comes from a vast subterranean lake which lies just below the surface of the dry ground all over northern Australia. You get it by boring down in much the same way as you do for oil; and these sub-artesian bores, with their windmills, each one lying ten or twenty miles from the next along the stock routes, dominate all life in the cattle country.

In the mustering season it's a splendid thing to see a mob of cattle working its way along these stock routes. They come over the horizon in a long line, one drover (the Australian word for cowboy) riding at the head, another at the rear, and perhaps a couple of others out on the flanks. As the cattle come across the plain, always moving from one bore to the next, you see first a yellow pillar of dust in the sky, and then you hear the voices of the drovers calling, 'Hey. Hey. Hey,' and the sound of the whips in the air, and you see the way they raise their arms in front of a stray animal that is turning away from the right direction. The line bunches, parts in the middle, then joins again and strings away across the plain. There is a kind of murmuring protest from the mob as it passes along. They travel about a thousand cattle at a time, and the object is always to lead them on to feed and water, but never to let them linger.

It is at night that most of the troubles occur, for cattle have the sort of nerves that would probably bring on ulcers in a city, and a sudden noise or an unexpected light in the darkness can start a stampede. The drovers take turns at riding round and round the mob till daylight comes; and as they ride they play mouth organs, sing songs and recite verses to the animals to reassure them that all is well and that there is nothing dangerous lurking beyond the camp-fires. One man I met had a repertoire ranging through grand opera to Keats's sonnets, and he was prepared at a pinch to produce passable rhyming verse of his own.

One poem the drovers know really well is an Australian ballad called 'The Man from Snowy River'; it is the story of a wild ride through the hills, and it has got just the right kind of hoof-beat in its rhythm:

Australian National Publicity Association

"It's a slow and unspectacular thing . . . they simply stand in
the bright sunshine, waiting." A calf, which was also destined
to die, standing beside its dead mother during a drought in
Northern Australia

There was movement at the station, for the word had
  passed around
That the colt from Old Regret had got away,
And had joined the wild bush horses—he was worth a
  thousand pound,
So all the cracks had gathered for the fray.

This kind of verse has got a calming effect, they say, on the cattle. But if some natural disaster happens in the night—a grass fire or a sheet of lightning—then no amount of poetry will do any good: the cattle are away in an instant and they will trample a sleeping man to death as they charge. Then they will run for miles in a bellowing mass and the only thing to do is to try and head them off so that they will turn in circles until at last they stop at the point where exhaustion becomes greater than fear.

A drover is paid according to the number and condition of the beasts he delivers at the railhead, and so a stampede is something of a disaster in his career; and in the Territory it's a point of professional pride never to lose a beast even on a journey of six weeks and two or three hundred miles.

Another kind of disaster, the worst of all, is drought. When drought hit the Northern Territories in 1952 there were something like a million cattle roaming over the plains. By the time I got there in June of that year they were dying in hundreds every week. It was not so much the water that failed—the subterranean lake is always available—but there was no feed on the ground and no hope of any unless rain fell.

There is nothing much to see in a drought; it's a slow and unspectacular thing. You ride on and on over the bare earth and there is absolutely nothing on the horizon ahead except the next windmill and the little groups of cattle standing knee deep in a mirage. When you come up to them they don't move. They simply stand in the bright sunshine, waiting. There is no noise of any kind, even when at last an animal gives up and sinks down on to its knees. Then, within the hour, the kites and the eagles arrive.

There is a kind of death-watch quality about the scene. Everything waits. After you have been living in the drought for a while any kind of noise or movement—a flock of cockatoos screeching round a windmill or the noise of a car engine—becomes an unnatural intrusion, and it has the effect of a discord or a sudden false note in music.

We saw a white mare on the move one day. She was only a bundle of skin and bones, but she had got some idea in her head—perhaps an instinctive memory of some place where grass normally grew—and she looked very fine indeed as she came trotting over the horizon, head up, mane flying, and apparently moving in a sure direction. All the other animals standing in the dust watched her go, impassively. There was, of course, no grass anywhere for a hundred miles, and the mare must have realized it, for she stopped suddenly, looked around uncertainly for a moment, and then stood silently with the other animals. They were all bound to die.

CHAPTER FOUR

In the Dreaming

DROUGHT or no drought the cattlemen hold a
race-meeting every year at a place called Brunette
Downs, one of the oldest and most famous stations on the
Barkly Tablelands, just south of the Gulf of Carpentaria.
They come in from five hundred miles around, pitch their
camps on the open plain, and then for the next three or
four days and nights they let themselves go. The proceed-
ings follow roughly upon the lines of a Texan rodeo, but
with one important difference: the introduction of the
Australian game of two-up. As a method of fast, simple,
cut-throat gambling, two-up probably has advantages over
poker or any other game; and the cattlemen love it with a
fierce passion. It is played, with variations, pretty nearly
everywhere in Australia, in the cities and the bush, and a
folk-lore which is strongly reminiscent of the world of
Damon Runyon has grown up around it. The game is
illegal, and in a large city like Sydney a two-up school will
operate at three or four places such as the loft of a garage
or the back rooms of a disused shop. One has to be a
friend of a regular member of the school in order to gain
admittance. At the entrance a door-keeper sits, known as
'the Cockatoo' because he tends to adopt a hunched-up
cockatoo-like position from having to sit for such long
hours in one place; he checks the credentials of the customers.

Two journalist friends of mine who were recently carrying out an inquiry into two-up signed themselves D. H.
Lawrence and James Joyce and gained admission to a

game in Sydney. They found themselves in a large bare room, with wooden benches set around and a padded canvas mattress on the floor. There were about twenty men in the room and one player held the 'kip'—a thin piece of wood a little wider and longer than a toothbrush—and on this two pennies were poised. He placed a £10 note on the floor and immediately this was 'covered' by two other players who each staked £5. Then the two pennies were tossed into the air. They fell noiselessly on the canvas mattress (the sound of pennies falling on bare boards has attracted the notice of the police before this), and landed with two heads upwards. This meant that the man with the kip collected the stake. When the pennies fell with two tails upward he lost, and if it was a head and a tail it was no game and he tossed again. The odds are always even, but there were many side-bets between those players who felt that there was a special run of luck in a certain direction.

According to the rules in this school the man with the kip was entitled to take half his money out after three consecutive winning tosses and then he went on for another three turns. If, on the other hand, he lost a toss he passed on the kip to his immediate neighbour in much the same way as the 'shoe' passes in baccarat or the dice in craps. The people who ran the school took ten per cent of the winnings and in return for this they not only fixed the meeting places but they bailed their customers out of gaol after a police raid, engaged legal counsel for them, and paid their fines. It was also an established custom that if a player won a considerable sum of money (and frequently a man will win £1,000 or more) and wished to go home, no one else was allowed to leave the building until he had been gone for half an hour.

The atmosphere is one of strong conspiratorial friendship, and one needs to be familiar with the jargon. A new player, for example, is known as a 'virgin'. One of my newspaper friends was a good deal startled when suddenly a cry went up: 'Give the virgin a go. Come on, Mr. Joyce.' Eager hands passed him the kip and the two pennies and in a moment he found himself involved in heavy betting. The pennies, incidentally, which are most favoured are those issued in the reign of King Edward the Seventh, since that monarch had an exceptionally large head which is quickly recognized. This side is polished and the other, the tail side, painted black. However, any penny will do, and the new coinage with Queen Elizabeth's head on it will shortly be in use.

This, then, is the game which is a ruling passion in Australia, and at the cattlemen's meeting at Brunette Downs (where the police were more indulgent) it was constantly being played in some corner of the paddock. In one short session I watched one man lose £1,250, and he did not appear to be unusually distressed. He kept a tally of his losses, and in the morning came bounding over the tussocks in a new limousine to the winner's camp with a cheque.

Betting on the horses was on a similar scale: these race-meetings are the one moment of the year when many of the cattlemen have any use for money, and they like to see it move fast from hand to hand. To work, to earn money, to lose it all in one glorious blow-out on beer and betting, and then to go back to work again; this is a repeated pattern in the north. A cattleman with a couple of hundred pounds in his pocket will quit his job, declaring that he is off to the city. But very often he never gets beyond the first pub, perhaps thirty miles away. This first whiff of a world of unlimited beer and bets is too much; and presently, when his money is gone, he comes back to the station looking for his job again. I do not say that this is general practice, but it does occur, and nowhere at any time did I ever hear of a cattleman regretting that he *had* 'gone on a burst'; they tended to recall the details lovingly as others perhaps might remember a honeymoon at Monte Carlo.

At Brunette certainly there was heavy gambling and homeric quantities of liquor were drunk, but these meetings are probably never as lurid as their reputations. I saw only one incident—a minor scuffle in the dance hall one night—and the offender was given the treatment which is customary in the Northern Territory: the police drove him seven miles out of camp and left him there to walk back.

Yet undeniably there used to be a tradition of violence in the north, perhaps not so much in the cattle country in the central areas, but further north in the true tropics around the port of Darwin. Certainly Darwin, for its short hundred-odd years of existence and its population of a few thousands, has a formidable record of homicide. Perhaps the heat has something to do with it (the Equator is only twelve degrees to the north), and it is a particularly humid heat during the summer rains, which are locally known as 'the wet'. Perhaps too the isolation is to blame; although Indonesia lies only four hundred miles away across the Timor Sea, there is no trade with Darwin, and the nearest Australian city of any size is well over a thousand miles away.

Often these murders are committed out of no really deep-seated motive, but haphazardly and for the most trivial reasons. It is almost as though men become suddenly seized with an intolerable feeling of frustration, like the *cafard* of the Foreign Legion. They feel they *must* break out into violent action to relieve the tension of monotony. Then, like one of the local storms which descend on Darwin without warning after a long succession of sunny days, the shooting begins.

There was just such a murder near Darwin when I was there. A boy in his early twenties killed a policeman, and it was in daylight and in the centre of a township. This boy had nothing against the policeman except a vague sort of grudge, but there was a race-meeting in the town that weekend, and he had been drinking. He came down the main street, shot the policeman from the hip, and then moved on slowly, menacing the other people in the street until he escaped out into the open bush. They searched for him through the night without success. In the morning, when they found him, his rage had evaporated. He sat on a fallen tree-trunk with his gun across his knees. A policeman walked up to him talking gently, took his gun away, and led him off. He was convicted of murder, eventually, in the Supreme Court.

There was no point in all this except its very pointlessness. It was the violence of sudden insane irritation, and of a childish contempt for the consequences. But the interesting thing was the reaction of the local people. They were appalled and angry; yet at the same time they said they understood it perfectly well. This boy had a grudge, and any man with a grudge, they argued, was liable to shoot. The idea of personal revenge still holds good in the north.

From the first this violence of the white man has bewildered and frightened the Australian aborigines; and finally it has ruined them. Less than a hundred years ago there were some 50,000 aborigines in the Northern Territory. Now there are barely 12,000 and most of these are gathered around Alice Springs and Darwin or the missions in the native territories.

The Australian aborigine is probably the father of us all; he is supposed by some people to be the nearest thing to the missing link, and the most primitive human being in existence. He tills no land, builds no house and, if you except his dogs, he has no domestic animals. In his wild state he counts up to two or three on his fingers, and after that it's 'a lot'. He goes quite naked and he eats raw kangaroo or lizard, occasionally tree grubs, and, when he can spear or net them, fish. He has no conception of private property—everything is shared—except that the tribal hunting areas are very strictly defined and there is a

system of taboos. At his tribal ceremonies (known as corroborees), he likes to deck himself out with mud and
feathers and to dance. He has no comprehension of history
or the future; all that is simply 'the dreaming'. In the
dreaming lie the strange and inexplicable things of life,
the stories of the old men, the dim communal memories of
the tribe, and the premonitions about what is going to
happen. The aborigine has no word for yesterday or tomorrow; only for today. Yesterday and tomorrow are in
the dreaming.

The white men burst into this slow-moving and
balanced scene a hundred years ago with the effect of a
nightmare. Since the aborigine was still living in the stone
age there was absolutely nothing in his dreaming to help
him comprehend even a horseman, let alone a great roaring flying-bird, bigger than the moon, with men inside it.
Equally there was the white man's hideous power to kill
at a great distance, his utterly incomprehensible interest
in getting useless stones out of the ground, and his strange
taboo that makes him want to keep everything he has for
himself.

For one hundred years the aborigine has been trying
desperately to catch up—to jump from the stone age
straight into the atomic age—and now, when he has almost
accomplished this it seems to be too late; his race has been
pretty well exterminated in the process.

The first Australian settlers never had a quarter as
much trouble from the aborigines as the American pioneers
had from the Red Indians. They simply used the aborigines
as they wanted them, as they used a horse or any other
animal. They moved into the native hunting grounds, took
what they wanted, and broke up the tribal system of life.
Just occasionally the aborigines made a wild and useless
protest by spearing a white man in his tent, but the re-
prisals were so horrible that the survivors lost heart and
crept away into the remote bush. On the whole the early

settlers were probably not deliberately unkind unless they were thwarted, but they paid the aborigines for their services in tobacco, sugar, scraps of clothing, and liquor, and these things, together with the breeding of the half-castes, were in the end as annihilating as a disease. It was a process which one missionary described as 'the tragedy of progress'.

For many years now there has been in Australia a strong conscience about the aborigines. Twenty-two per cent of the Northern Territory has been set aside as their exclusive hunting grounds, and no white can enter there without permission. But this was like giving a dog a kennel in the yard after he has got used to sleeping in the house. The aborigine now likes sugar and tobacco, he likes wearing clothes and the life of the town. For him all the business of boomerangs and spears and the eating of cold lizard is turning back the clock. He prefers to take a job as a mechanic in a garage, or better still no regular job at all, just a little odd fetching and carrying for the white man, enough to enable him to live and sit in the sunshine outside the pub with his fine new sombrero hat down over his eyes.

It is getting hard to find a genuine corroboree these days, although only a few years ago you could hear singing and dancing in the encampments every night. They used to act out simple little scenes; the hunting of a kangaroo, the coming of rain, the things they felt about a birth or a death or a marriage in the tribe. Not long ago it was announced that native women, known as lubras, were entitled to the government maternity bonus. One of the cattle-station owners, a man with a genuine interest in the aborigines on his property, asked the lubras how they wanted to spend the money. They wanted gramophones, and the music they liked best was hill-billy. *Comin' round the Mountain* is a favourite, and they play that now, night after night, instead of making corroboree.

But the tragedy of progress is not, as yet, quite complete. Every year the aborigines in the white settlements feel some vague kind of stirring, something out of the dreaming, which they cannot resist. Then they go walkabout. They announce one day to their employers that they will be gone a little while—perhaps two weeks, perhaps a month or more—and then they are off. They throw off their clothes and walk out naked into the bush, carrying a boomerang and spear. They seem to head in no particular direction and without any definite object in view; they walk simply to appease a natural restlessness, and they live as their ancestors did by what they can hunt. Often they take a course which leads them in a wide circle, but in any event they always come back with the same fidelity of a stockbroker returning to his office from a fishing holiday in the mountains. Then they put on their clothes again and slide back into civilization.

Yet even here a change is on the way. The manager of one of the big cattle stations told me that when some of his native stockmen went walkabout last year they took suitcases with them, and they started off by hopping a ride on a passing motor lorry. They were away a month, and then came back by passenger airline.

Clearly it is too late to have regrets about all this; one might just as well have regrets about one's own lost adolescence. Even those people who really love the aborigines and who have fought a losing battle on their behalf for the last half century are beginning to accept the view that they are bound to go the same way as the North American Red Indians. Some of them on the cattle stations (they make the finest horsemen, and few of the larger stations could get along without them) have great dignity and energy in their bearing, and these, no doubt, will find a place in the new order of things. For the rest only death lies in the dreaming.

The half-castes are another problem and a worse one.

Information Service Australia House, London

A lubra beside a water-hole in Central Australia

At present there are about 30,000 of them in Australia, but the number is steadily increasing. It is the ancient tragedy of men wandering in limbo between two social worlds, and there is nothing particularly new about its appearance in Australia except that here you can see the whole unhappy story developing from its beginnings. In New Zealand, where the Maoris are of a very much higher civilization than the Australian natives, the matter has been solved brilliantly. There was a series of bitter skirmishes when the white settlers first arrived, and then, stage by stage, the Maoris were absorbed into the white society. Today there are Maoris in the New Zealand parliament and in all the professions; and it is even a matter of some pride for a New Zealander to have Maori blood in his veins. In Australia, meanwhile, things have moved precisely in the other direction.

The white invaders took the native girls as they took them everywhere else in the world, and the girls themselves were glad enough to have a white man's baby; it was a distinction of a kind, it meant food and clothes, and it set the girl a little above the other members of her tribe. The elders might have deplored it, but there was nothing they could do. Usually there was no marriage, and the natives knew nothing about the white man's marriage ritual anyway. And now these thirty-thousand half-castes hang about the bush towns, trying to find a place for themselves in a society where they are not accepted. They tend to be more black than white and in the first generation, at any rate, their features have a definitely aboriginal cast. In the bush towns they go to school with the white children and they are not less intelligent; it is when they go home each afternoon to their squalid wooden shanties in the native part of the town that the sense of inferiority is forced upon them; and this becomes more open and more real as they grow into adolescence. They feel, naturally, that they must make a fight not to slip back into the primitive life of their black ancestors, but when they try to thrust themselves into the white man's society they find there a system of taboos as strong as anything in the native past they have left behind. They struggle for a while and then, usually, they give up. Either they marry among themselves or they lose heart entirely and sink back gradually into the life of the native encampments.

There is nothing very dramatic about this, it is a slow and fairly painless evil; the hopeless and haphazard cycle rolls on from day to day relieved by a gesture and a kind word here and there, and as yet there have been no riots. The problem is still so small that nobody bothers about it very much, and I doubt whether I myself would ever have noticed it but for a friend, an Englishman, who now lives in Australia.

This man—I think I must simply call him X—believed himself to be the last of the Xs; with him the family name dies out. He was therefore a good deal intrigued one day when he saw in a Melbourne paper a paragraph stating that the wife of a certain William X, a drover, had given birth to a child while she and her husband were taking a mob of cattle across the northern plains.

In the winter of 1952 my friend X travelled with me on my trip to the north, and he at once began to make inquiries about his namesake. In Alice Springs nobody had any information, which was strange in that country where distance means nothing and every man is a distinct personality known for a thousand miles around. As we went north we kept on inquiring at all the wayside townships, but it was not until we got to a particularly remote spot on the edge of the tropics—it was a battered wooden store in a wilderness of mulga scrub—that the man behind the counter nodded and said yes, he knew William X. And he added sourly, 'He won't come back here any more.'

We asked, mildly, why not.

'Too many puppies.'

Information Service Australia House, London

Two aborigines going walkabout

We got this translated (it means too many bad debts), and the storekeeper went on to state that he considered young William X to be a drunkard, a swindler, and a very bad character indeed.

We went on then to the next police station some fifty miles up the road, and there they also knew William X quite well. But they thought the storekeeper had exaggerated. William was not a bad lad, they said. He was a wonderful drover, a horseman who could break in any wild brumby from the plains, and he seemed to have some special understanding of cattle. Usually he was in great demand in the droving season, but it was some months since they had seen him. Possibly he was down at Djarra —the policeman waved his hand towards the void. Djarra was a thousand miles away.

A couple of weeks later we found ourselves at the mining town of Mount Isa, not far from Djarra—a mere hundred miles. But the road was appalling and our time was running out. We found a taxi-driver in Mount Isa who in his spare time flew an ancient Fox Moth as a hobby, and he agreed to take us down to Djarra. There was just room for the three of us in the plane, and we travelled not much faster than a modern car over a landscape which is as lonely and moonlike as the deserts of Africa. At Djarra, a collection of iron and wooden shanties in endless space, there were two mobs—one of cattle and the other of goats—grazing across the flat space that served as a landing field. We dived and scared the goats off first, and then turned and dived on the cattle. Then we came into a dusty tussocky landing and walked into the town. At the police station they looked at us with some surprise when we asked about William X; but they said we would find him in the pub. We had a certain feeling of elation then as we went through the swing doors of the public bar. And there, leaning against the counter, drunk, and with an exceedingly black skin, stood the last of the Xs.

He was a boy of twenty-three or twenty-four with very thick black, curly hair, a cattleman's wide-brimmed hat on the back of his head, and he was wearing a coloured shirt and tattered trousers. His high-heeled elastic-sided boots had split across the insteps. He was very dirty and not very cheerful.

He achieved, however, a grunted 'Good day' as we came in, and my friend X asked him if he would like a drink. William at once tossed off the remains of his gin and held forward his empty glass.

I do not think that at that moment my friend was particularly relishing the conversation that lay ahead, but he tackled it manfully. 'Is your name William X?' he asked.

'Yes.'

'Funny thing,' said X, 'so is mine.'

Then the boy smiled. It was a charming smile, very white teeth in the dark aboriginal face, and presently he began to talk easily and pleasantly in a soft, slightly hesitant voice.

He was born, he thought, in Alice Springs. He had never seen his parents; he had simply been told that his father was white and his mother black. As a boy he had been educated and cared for by a white family in Alice Springs, but they too had vanished out of his life, and in some way he had kept himself going with odd jobs on the cattle stations. He had grown up with horses and cattle, and he loved them. At eighteen he had become a drover in his own right, one of the best (this we confirmed later on from the people in the town). He had never had a drink until the year before, and he had never been out of a job. What started his drinking? He didn't know. Something to do with his marriage, he said vaguely.

It was indeed, as we found out later, a great deal to do with his marriage. He had married in the only way that was open to him, into a family half-native, and half half-caste, and his wife's relatives were illiterate, squalid, and hopelessly poor. Little by little they had engulfed him. He found himself living not only with his wife but with all her family as well, and in the native way, sleeping on sacking on the floor, eating with his hands.

Young William did not seem to me to be a very strong character, and perhaps he had not put up much of a struggle. Still one could see his point; it cannot have been very easy living in a family where only he could read or write. Nothing the white men had taught him had been of much use in the end. He had no one to talk to.

He put all this to us without complaint, but with a kind of easy fatalism; it had to happen, he said. What the hell? Now he was out of a job and on the way to becoming a souse. And he asked us to join him in another gin.

It was, on the whole, a commonplace little tragedy, but my friend X is a kindly character. Perhaps he was most affected, as I was, by the fact that this boy had had a glimpse of pride and independence, when he was one of the finest horsemen in the north and game to take on any mob of cattle, however wild they were and however bad the drought. At all events, X was making certain arrangements when I left Australia. He was moving young William down to Alice Springs with his wife and baby, but without the rest of the family. He was advancing him some hundreds of pounds so that he could build a house, and he had found him a job. By now, I imagine, the last of the Xs must be getting back on to his feet again.

And yet one wonders if there is any real answer to William or any of the other thirty thousand who were born into the half-world of the half-caste. In Australia there is an abiding fear of the coloured races; the Japanese so nearly came and destroyed them last time. Barely nine million people of white European stock (they number less than the populations of London or New York) perch on the edges of a vast and empty island, and sooner or later when you are there you are made conscious of the teeming millions of coloured people just a day's flight to the north, in the East Indies and China. What is to stop them coming south in the next war? And what is a half-caste in Australia but a sort of fifth columnist waiting for the day? Australians don't say this, nor perhaps even consciously do they think it; but the vague suspicion is there, the bourgeois distrust of the inferior race; and it will outlaw young William to the day he dies, however well he rides a horse.

I asked my friend X before I left if he really had known nothing of William's origins.

'Well,' he said, 'there was an uncle in our family, a doctor, who was supposed to be rather a wild character. He came out to Australia from England some time last century. But we never heard what became of him, or what he did when he got here.'

CHAPTER FIVE

The Bitumen

O N my journey through the Northern Territory I did
what nearly every other traveller does—I drove up
the highway which runs from Alice Springs northwards to
Darwin. It is an astonishing road. For half a century
various Australian governments have made plans and
argued about it, but nothing much was done until 1942.
Then, abruptly, it was realized that the Japanese were
moving down fast through the Dutch East Indies, and
clearly Australia was the next target. It seemed quite
likely that they would land at Darwin (which they were
already destroying from the air), and then spread south-
wards before General Macarthur could even get his armies
into position to meet them. Then, at some speed, Australian and American engineers moved into the Northern
Territory and built the Stuart Highway at a cost of five
million pounds.

It follows pretty much along the original route taken
by Stuart on his overland journey on horseback in 1862,
that is to say it runs for 950 miles, mostly in a straight
line, and although it was named after Stuart the local
people always call it 'The Bitumen'. They have a way of
identifying places in that vast space by saying they are
'East (or West) of the bitumen', or simply 'Up (or down)
the bitumen', in much the same way as you might orientate
stars in the sky from the Milky Way.

An enthusiast in a sports car once covered the distance
in ten hours (he hit a kangaroo on the way and it disinte-
grated over the bonnet); but most people prefer to take

three days on the journey. There is no traffic to speak of
and no towns on the route, only a bush pub or a little
collection of wooden and iron houses every hundred miles
or so; you just drive and drive.

Not so long ago a young English doctor and his wife
died of thirst on this road when their car broke down; they
were new to these spaces and they did not realize that the
car radiator was still full of water which would have kept
them alive for another couple of days. Walking, in the
midsummer heat, gets you nowhere; you can manage
barely a dozen miles before you collapse. The trick is
always to carry extra water tanks and always stay with
your vehicle; sooner or later someone will come along,
even if it is only a roaming family of natives or a drover
with a mob of cattle on the move.

These things give you a mild sense of adventure as you
drive out of Alice Springs. It is rather like setting out on
a voyage in a small open boat. The sameness of the sea is
repeated here in the unending plains of anthills and mulga
scrub; and the black surface of the road stretches ahead of
you apparently for ever. It has a mesmerizing effect. But
then, suddenly the bush is apt to become alive. A flock
of cockatoos rises up screaming from a waterhole. A mob
of wild horses breaks across the track, stirring up many
other living things that lurk on the hot ground: the wild
dogs known as dingoes, the lizards, and the bush turkeys.
Possibly you catch sight of a euro—an animal which is
much the same as a kangaroo except that it has hair
instead of fur and is darker in colour. The euro stares for
a moment with a gentle kind of wonder, poised upright on
his tail and his back legs, and then goes bounding off
through the rocks. If it is a female there is often a joey, a
young one, riding in her pouch or pounding along un-
steadily behind. After this the complete silence and im-
movability of the bush closes in again and there is
nothing to look at but the road.

Death is an antiseptic thing in this dry hot air, and you are always conscious of it in one form or another. Usually it's a dead wallaby or a kangaroo—they get bewildered and dash into the car headlights at night. In the morning the kites and the eagles gather over the dead body. They wait on the ground until your car is a quarter of a mile away and then rise up in lazy circles. If you stop they continue circling, all day if necessary. Then as soon as you are gone they swoop again. Between the eagles, the dingoes and the hot sun it is only a little time before the dead kangaroo is another heap of white bones and dry leather on the roadway, and soon the white ants will advance and demolish that too.

Your first overnight stop is a gold-mining township called Tennant Creek, which enjoyed a brief spell of glory in the newspapers some years ago when the miners got tired of digging in the hard rock and began rioting among themselves. The local storekeeper still tells you, with a touch of pride, that no man has ever died a natural death within the town limits. Latterly, however, the miners' high spirits seem to have been lost in wealth, and the roar of modern machinery (they send away about three hundred thousand pounds' worth of gold each year). The gaol was empty when I was there.

After Tennant Creek it's much the same thing again for another four hundred miles until you reach Katherine, where you begin to touch the edge of the tropics. About this point you become uneasily aware of the anthills. For the past seven hundred miles they have been marching steadily beside you. Down at The Alice they were just little nondescript mounds scattered through the gum trees. Around Tennant Creek they were standing two feet high above the ground, and they stretched away in millions to the horizon like a petrified forest of sawn-off tree trunks. Now, at Katherine, they have grown to a monstrous and impossible size, at least eight feet in height and thickness, and each one is shaped like a Gothic cathedral, with the nave always running on a north–south line and with long ridges like buttresses reaching to the ground.

In the moonlight these anthills can give you an eerie feeling. They are so silent and motionless; never a sign of the actual white ants themselves. But then you remember their deadly voracity; they have been known to eat the inside out of billiard balls and they can bring a house down in a few months. And you remember, too, those innumerable anthills behind you, always getting bigger and bigger. Then you can quite easily be seized with an illusion that you are being watched and followed; that the ants are going to come and get you too in the end.

Australia has had some spectacular successes in dealing with pests, mostly by working on the principle of setting a pest to destroy a pest. When the prickly pear was sweeping across the grazing land at the rate of hundreds of miles a year they imported from America an insect called the cactoblastis which enjoys a diet of prickly pear to the exclusion of all else; and before long there was no prickly pear trouble in Australia. In the same way when the rabbits became intolerable (they were the descendants of a few pairs brought in to feed the early colonists last century), the scientists found a mosquito which was apparently designed by nature with the express purpose of destroying rabbits.

But nothing yet has been found game enough to tackle the white ant. He keeps on munching away through the centuries, unimpeded by droughts, fires, diseases, or anything else. His ultimate object, clearly, is to eat the world.

However, it is only dead or inanimate things that the white ant will attack, and from Katherine onward to your journey's end in Darwin everything is brilliantly alive. It is the more remarkable since you have travelled for so long through the empty wastes in the centre, where even a windmill or a bushman's shack is a sensation to the eye.

Information Service Australia House, London

"They have grown to a monstrous and impossible size, at least 8 feet in height and thickness and each one is shaped like a Gothic Cathedral." Anthills on the road to Darwin

Here, in the far north, the rivers reminded me of the descriptions in R. M. Ballantyne's books about the tropics which I used to read as a boy, especially the one called *Martin Rattler*. Immense bamboos shoot up from the edges of the pools, and sometimes there are mango trees that trail long cords of flowering creepers from their topmost branches. There is a solid humid heat that gets into your bones, and birds fly about in such numbers above the jungle pools that you might think they were trapped there as in an aviary in a zoo. And in the green silent water below the crocodiles are waiting.

One day we stopped for lunch on the river just outside Katherine. We had been driving since soon after dawn and there had been only two breaks in the journey; once when I stalked a bush turkey with a camera (but it quickened its pace and hurried away like a man being followed in a crowd), and once again when we took a pot-shot at a wild dog. There is a reward of £1 for every dog you kill (they attack the sheep and other animals), so when we saw the lean, ginger body in the scrub and the two pert, triangular ears, we got down from the car with a rifle. The wild dog or the dingo is one of the few animals in Australia which does not move you with a sense of its helplessness. The dingo watches you with a kind of furtive truculence, and as the shot rang out, well wide of the mark, this one went off through the bush with an easy, confident lope, and it seemed to me that he was unafraid, even contemptuous.

So now, having travelled nearly three hundred miles in the morning we were a little tired, and we sat beside the edge of the pool, drinking rum and water and eating cold beetroot sandwiches. Neither of us spoke; it was a pleasure to sit there in the green shade letting the minutes tick by in silence. Then, gradually, the eye took note of all the things that were happening around us in the jungle. A superb grey ibis, as slender and elegant as a Greek vase, perched on a paper-bark tree on the other side of the river.

He was quite motionless. He took no notice of the little honey-birds with long needle beaks and delicate colour on their breasts that kept zig-zagging back and forth. There were hooded crows, very slow flyers, with a splash of scarlet under their wings, circling all about him; but his eye was fastened intently upon the striped fish darting about in the river. He was on the point of diving at last, when accidentally I rustled the paper round the beetroot sandwiches. Deciding at once that this danger was more important than his hunger, the ibis spread his wings and flew away.

If there were crocodiles in the river or kangaroos and emus in the jungle behind us we did not see them, but the longer we sat there in silence the more we felt that they were there, watching us, waiting to see what we would do. Presently a crane came by, an absurd bird, with a six-foot wing span, trailing two match-stick legs behind it, apart and parallel. It circled about very high up, caught sight of us, and then glided off slowly to the next lagoon. After that we did see, for an instant, three wallabies peering at us across the spinifex grass, but they came no nearer, and presently we too got up and went away.

Only once before, very long ago, at dusk in the zoo at Khartoum in Africa, can I remember wild birds and animals drawing round me in just this way, more with curiosity than with fear; and it leaves one with the odd and soothing feeling that a benediction has been given.

When we were in Darwin, X and I went out to one of the nearer cattle stations where, they said, wild buffalo were roaming. We had heard great things of the buffalo shooting. It is not the meat that is wanted; this is good enough for eating but it quickly turns bad in that heat, and there is no means of getting it to a refrigeration plant. It is the buffalo hides, sometimes an inch thick, that the hunters seek, and in a normal year each hide brings around £12. (You will frequently see advertisements in the

Darwin from the air

Darwin papers: 'Best prices paid for buffalo hides, peanuts,
and crocodiles.')

They hunt buffalo on horseback, and the method is to
ride straight into a mob while it is on the run and single
out the bulls (it is illegal to kill the cows). A good man
will ride right up alongside a bull and put a bullet through
the base of his skull while he is still at full gallop. A team
of aborigines follows on behind to skin the carcases. It's
an exciting sport that can turn dangerous if the bull is not
killed at once but only wounded; then he will stand and
charge.

X and I were received a little guardedly at the station
homestead until we made it clear that we had come not to
shoot, but to look. Then the manager offered us a guide,
and he raised his voice towards the native encampment:
'Billee.' A blackfellow emerged from his hut, infinitely
tired. 'You-fella,' roared the manager, 'you look-um
find-um Billee.' Just why this gibberish should be more
intelligible to the natives than straight English is one of
the mysteries of the north; but apparently it succeeds just
as baby-talk is supposed to succeed with very small children. Perhaps it's the tone of voice that counts. Billee,
however, was not there—he had gone walkabout, they
said, which may have been another way of saying that he
too was fatigued in that oppressive midday heat—and in
the end the manager came with us himself.

We drove off then, over a rough bush track to the
buffalo country and the lagoons. These lagoons are simply
wonderful. They lie there, warm, fetid, and muddy, perhaps a mile or more in circumference, in the heart of the
jungle, and they spawn with life in a way that makes you
think you are in the presence of the beginning of the world
when everything was a teeming swamp. Bright fields of
flowering lilies cover the margins of the lake, and among
these the cranes and the ibis and the storks pick their way
sedately, lifting one delicate webbed foot after another,

and always with the long, down-pointing beak held ready
to dart in among the lily roots for a frog or a fish. The
pelicans come zooming in for a crash-landing in the centre
of the lake, and in the trees the galahs, the cornellas, and
the lurid cockatoos set up a constant caterwauling as they
move in flocks from one part of the bank to another.

I never saw so many birds at one time. The geese and
the duck light down in tens of thousands, so that all the
surface of the water is covered with little bouncing dots.
Then, when you draw near, they take off together, with a
noise which I can only describe as a rapid patter-patter-
patter, and in such numbers that, for a moment, they
darken the sun. The manager told me that on the stations
the white men do not bother to shoot the ducks; when they
need fresh game they send out a native boy with a gun and
a couple of cartridges; and I believed him when he said
that with two shots the boy was expected to bring home
three or four birds at least.

In a good season the pelicans go far south, and they like
to lie in the green grass. But in a drought they come
swarming back towards the coast in thousands, looking
for water. 'We had a plague of pelicans once,' the manager
said, 'we had to poison them.' Then there are the huge
fish called barramundi, which in the dry season can keep
alive in the mud for months, and the wild horses that run
in hundreds through this country, and the tree-pythons,
and the hissing four-foot lizards called goannas, which the
natives love to eat, and which run on short bent legs with
a lurching wobbly motion very much like a child's mechanical toy.

Except for the birds none of these creatures exactly
thrust themselves on your attention. A hundred years ago
when the blackfellow with his boomerang and spear was
their only enemy, they swarmed. But nowadays you have
to stand very still in the bush to see the wild animals, or
move so rapidly that you take them by surprise.

An aborigine with his spear fitted into a woomera

We came on the buffaloes about a mile beyond the lagoons, and the first sight of them was rather an anti-climax. There they stood, eight or nine of them, quietly grazing on the edge of a clearing, the big bull with his downward-curving horns, and the cows stolidly following on behind. My first impression was that they were very dirty, very ugly, and quite exceptionally mild. The bull was the timid one. As soon as we got out of the car with our cameras he lifted his head and moved towards the trees. When we stopped, he stopped. When we moved to the left he moved to the right. The cows stood around in a circle observing this ballet with quiet, incurious eyes. In the end we all stood still, looking at one another, as immovable as chess players, waiting for the next move. After a minute or two the bull began to fidget again. He turned his two-ton rump towards me (I was standing about thirty yards away), looked at me over his shoulder, and I took a picture. That click was too much for his strained nerves. He threw up his head and bolted for the pandanus palms. Immediately the cows started bolting too, indeed we all bolted, and even at the time I remember thinking that the whole scene was quite remarkably silly.

We spent a full hour stalking these and other buffaloes, always trying to keep on the leeward side, away from their sharp noses; but I never did get nearer than twenty or thirty yards. Alas for my photographs. Those dark spots near the top right-hand corner are the buffaloes, the largest and wildest animals in the whole continent of Australia. And if you observe closely you will see that they are for ever running away.

All this area—it is the big hump of Australia on the Arafura Sea—was the part where the Japanese were expected to land, and MacArthur placed about a hundred thousand soldiers there once the Stuart Highway was built. The Japanese never arrived, and the men never had to fight a battle on Australian soil, but at least they did

Information Service Australia House, London

"The black surface of the road stretches ahead of you apparently for ever." The Bitumen, the highway that runs for nearly a thousand miles from Alice Springs to Darwin

succeed for a year or two in breaking up the loneliness of
the north. When the war was over many of the soldiers
declared that they were going to come back with their
families and open up this wonderful country where bananas
and pawpaws—in fact anything at all—seemed to leap out
of the ground and bear fruit within a few months of plant-
ing. But they never did come back. There are actually
fewer people in the Northern Territory now than there
were before the war. Somehow it has all been too difficult
and too distant.

It is a mournful business these days, driving the last
hundred miles into Darwin and seeing how much has gone
to waste. The roads the army built lead off nowhere into
the empty bush. Every few miles you come on mouldering
huts and the wooden skeletons of hundreds of tents; and
occasionally there is an abandoned aircraft falling to bits
among the trees. From year to year the jungle creeps
steadily over it all and the white ants are at work. Even
the airfields in moderately good repair have the sort of
desolation that clings to a summer holiday place in the
winter-time, except that the effect is redoubled here because
the neglect is permanent.

A railway runs beside the road for a few hundred miles
south of Darwin, and there were once great hopes about
that too. It was supposed to link up with the railhead at
Alice Springs, seven hundred miles to the south, but somehow everyone connected with it lost heart. The line finishes
in a place called Birdum, but nobody lives there now. Just
occasionally, after an interval of days, an ancient nine-
teenth-century locomotive comes rattling down the track
with a line of weathered cars or trucks behind it. Time
does not count for very much. If you chance to see a
couple of stork-like birds called brolgas dancing beside a
waterhole, or some other entertainment in the bush, the
obliging engine-driver will stop the train for a bit while
the passengers get out and look.

Darwin itself is a kind of white man's Singapore. There is an antiseptic flavour about these houses built on stilts (for coolness), the wide streets, the officials in starched shirts and shorts, the bars and the soda fountains. It is as though the Anglo-Saxons were trying to keep the East at bay, which indeed they are.

The town, and it is only a small place of a few thousand people, has recovered from the worst of the Japanese air-raids, but you can still see the half-sunken wrecks in the harbour. Some of the ships were American, and nothing was done about them until a few years ago when a young Canadian named Carl Atkinson bought them, as they lay on the sea bed, from the United States government. Atkinson is a man of small boats and the sea, and as a physical spectacle he comes about as close to an Ernest Hemingway character as you could wish to see. He had a short and successful brush with the Australian authorities who wanted him to pay customs duty on anything he salvaged, and then he got to work. Apparently oblivious of sharks, Portuguese men-o'-war, a painful infection known as Coral Ear, and the other dangers of the tropical sea, he dives through the cool corridors of his wrecks and brings up wonderful things. His yard on a strip of the beach outside Darwin is littered with a Robinson Crusoe collection of barrels, ropes, lifebuoys, sea-chests, binnacles, chairs, and ironwork. He has even fished an entire Chevrolet car out of the sea. Recently his household complained that they had no presentable china dinner service. Atkinson dived down and got them one.

His companions under the sea are the pearl divers who have been coming to Darwin from Malaya and Japan since the nineteenth century. Nowadays it is not the pearls which are sought—they are usually given to the divers as a kind of bonus—it is the mother-of-pearl of the shell itself. This is the stuff from which most of the shirt buttons of the world are made. Since the war the Japanese have not been allowed back into Australian waters, but the Malays have returned, deft, handsome little men for whom life is still so hard that they think it well worth risking every day. Not long before I arrived in Darwin three of them were brought gasping and nearly dead to the surface when the compressed-air pumps failed on one of the luggers. They lay on the deck for three days until they recovered; then they went down again.

By the early nineteen-fifties none of these enterprises, not the pearling, the gold-mining, or even the cattle industry, had made any real headway in breaking the hoodoo on the north and getting the country populated. People were still drifting away to the big cities in the south. It looked as though the north was due for another of its chronic downslides into neglect and economic depression. It even seemed that the land might return again to the wild animals and the bush and the few remaining natives who have survived the tragedy of progress. And this was the point where uranium came on to the scene.

CHAPTER SIX

The Jungle

PROSPECTING for gold and other precious minerals in Australia is, I suppose, not so different anywhere else. That is to say it is like gambling: there is a kind of insanity in it. Once a man has got the urge to go prospecting in his blood then there are no limits to what he will do, and not much reason either. He must go on and on; he can never have enough. He might start out with dreams of sudden wealth and of how he will spend it once he gets it, but if he is a true prospector that vision will become, unconsciously, less and less important; it is the pursuit that really counts, the suspense and the hope.

Like a true gambler he must always risk a little more than he can afford, and he must always test himself a little beyond the normal powers of endurance. Failure is never the end: it is simply the point of departure for a new expedition. The exquisite moment, the justification of it all, happens when the poor man, having lost hope a dozen times, really does come upon the promise of something. It may be nothing but a speck of yellow at the bottom of his dollying pan, a gleam in a chunk of rock, but for him all Eldorado lies beyond. He has not yet quite got his hands on it, but it's there, just ahead of him. This gleam of gold is the first messenger, and he flings himself into the search in a frenzy, he forgets entirely about himself, about food and time, night or day. He is utterly obsessed; and this, one imagines, is as good a glimpse of happiness as anyone can hope for this side of paradise. At all events it is this moment of bright hope, and the repeated memories of it, that keeps the prospector alive from one barren year to the next. He remains, as a rule, rather a solitary creature but very tough and self-reliant; and for we children who were brought up in Australia the prospector had an aura which never glowed around the other grown-ups who had taken safe jobs in the city.

All prospectors were personified for me by my great-uncle Bill. He was a hopeless case. The other lunatics who went bush with a pick and a shovel and a swag over their shoulders usually came back with *something*, if it was only a half-interest in a gravel pit; but Uncle Bill never. He went through the most fearful privations and dangers in the unexplored west and the far north, but in the end it was not Uncle Bill who found gold—it was the other uncles who had stayed behind in Melbourne and set up nice comfortable businesses in wool-brokering and the grocery trade.

We children adored Uncle Bill. He must have been about fifty-five when I first remember him. He was riddled with arthritis, too old to go prospecting any more, and one of my prosperous merchant-uncles had made the gesture of setting him up in a chicken run at a place called Mitcham, just outside Melbourne. Uncle Bill lived alone in a wooden bungalow with pitch-pine ceilings, looking after the chickens and the apple orchard, and we children were occasionally taken up there for our holidays.

He seemed to us to be a man of infinite resource. He not only cooked his own meals in a black iron pot, but he could light a fire in the native fashion by rubbing two sticks together. He knew all about snakes and sometimes killed them for us. He forecast the weather with one glance at the sky, and once he concocted a home-brewed beer of yeast and sarsaparilla roots which made us all both sick and tipsy. He knew that in certain months of the year the fearsome Australian bull-ants would not bite, and while we stood around awe-struck in a circle he put his old gnarled hands down on the ground and let the ants crawl up his arm and under his shirt. Sometimes he would make little concertinas of paper that looked like white caterpillars, and if you dropped water on them they would crawl along the table in a wonderfully lifelike way. But best of all we loved to hear his stories.

There was the time up in the Kimberleys when he had missed The Welcome Nugget by only a couple of feet; Uncle Bill had abandoned his digging but another fellow came along, sank the shaft a little further and was rich for life. Once he had nearly died of thirst in horrible agony— but he watched the flight of a wild pigeon and he had just enough strength to follow until he came upon a native waterhole. He had actually seen Ned Kelly, the great bushranger who robbed the gold coaches, and back in the 'eighties once he had lived for six months on kangaroo meat and nothing else. The most dreadful experience of all had happened one night when Uncle Bill was encamped alone, hundreds of miles from anywhere, beyond Kalgoorlie in the west. He woke in the darkness and saw, just a few inches above his head, the point of a native spear piercing the roof of his tent. He watched while the spear made a little rip in the canvas. Then it was withdrawn and a native eye glared down on him. Uncle Bill reached for his gun and fired point blank through the canvas. There was a demoniacal yell and then silence. Uncle Bill sat up all night with his gun cocked (he had only one cartridge left), but he heard nothing more; and in the morning there were traces of blood on the ground.

This was the point when my mother would tell Uncle Bill that he ought to be ashamed of himself—he was scaring the children to death—and she used to bundle me to bed, assuring me that all his stories were false, he had just 'made them up'. This, of course, did not prevent me from waking sometimes in the night, and then the knots in the pitch-pine ceiling above my head assumed menacing and alarming shapes, like the murderous eye of a wild head-hunter looking down on me. My mother would come hurrying in to quieten me when I sobbed in terror, and after that Uncle Bill would tell no more stories for the next few days.

But his stories were not false, or at any rate if they did not happen to him personally, then they certainly happened to others, and much worse stories than these. Death through thirst, or exhaustion, or murder was no uncommon thing on the goldfields in those days.

When, finally, I was taken to a gold-mine it was a fearful disappointment. No blackfellows. No snakes. No kangaroos. Nothing but a vast pile of roaring machinery and a mountain of dun-coloured, boring stone. Prosaic office buildings with trams and traffic running past the door. It is the same now with all the great mining giants in Australia. Companies like the Broken Hill Proprietary and Mount Isa have become commercial empires worth many millions of pounds. They have erected whole cities in the bush, great steelworks, railways, and shipbuilding yards, and their shares are quoted in London and New York. Yet all of them began not so very long ago when Uncle Bill and his fellow dreamers went out alone into unexplored country with their picks and shovels. They were the people who first found these reefs of gold, silver, lead, zinc, and copper. Big business came in behind them and created the Eldorados.

But the prospectors are not quite finished yet. They survive, a case-hardened and timeless group in the north, and it was just such a man as Uncle Bill who discovered uranium at Rum Jungle.

Already it is getting a little difficult to separate the truth from the legends about Rum Jungle. It seems certain, however, that the field is fabulously rich, perhaps the richest uranium deposit in the world, and as yet no one knows how far or how deep the field extends. New satellite fields are being discovered as far as sixty miles away. People, in fact, are beginning to see a vision of the north which is quite as bright as anything that Stuart imagined when he first arrived there on his horse in 1862.

The early history of the place is rather a tangle. It seems that soon after Stuart made his report, the South Australian government was seized with the idea of opening up the land and forming a new colony. An area round Rum Jungle, roughly forty by sixty miles, was arbitrarily marked out and divided into blocks each of half a square mile. Any man who cared to come north into the wilderness was promised one of these blocks free; indeed, the government was so anxious to attract people that every prospective settler was not only granted the land in perpetual freehold but all the mining rights as well.

There was a mild boom for a while. A few shiploads of adventurers arrived and claimed their blocks of land, but very few of them tried to cultivate the soil. Many of the new owners never even visited their properties before they became disillusioned with the north and drifted away to the south again.

For the next sixty or seventy years then, the land was abandoned to the aborigines and the occasional prospectors who came fossicking about through the bush, mostly in search of gold. They found no gold at Rum Jungle, but they did find tin and copper, and you can still see the primitive shafts they dug in the rock.

Up to this point the place was known simply as The Jungle, and a small settlement developed there. A storekeeper came out from Darwin to supply the miners with the basic needs of life: tea, sugar, flour, salt, preserved meat, tobacco, and liquor. For a while things went happily enough; the work was profitable and the miners paid for their stores with straight tin. But then the ore petered out, and when the shafts became flooded there was no machinery to pump them dry. Any amount of uranium was lying about, but nobody was interested in it then and they left it in the ground.

After a while the storekeeper refused to give the miners any further credit, and they must have been fairly desperate, for they broke into the store one night. They ignored the sugar and the flour and went directly to a barrel of rum; and in their eagerness they smashed the cask. The liquor at once flowed out of the store and down a slope into a spring, where it mingled with the fresh water and made a convenient mixture there. In the morning the miners were discovered happily lapping up the miraculous draught from the pool; and from that moment The Jungle has always been Rum Jungle.[1]

After this nothing whatever happened to Rum Jungle for many years. At intervals it was awakened from its long sleep when the overland telegraph line and the road were constructed, when the abortive railway line was put in, and again, much later, when the soldiers made their brief stay in the Second World War. But by the end of the nineteen-forties Rum Jungle had returned to its natural solitude again. Then in 1949 Jack White appeared.

White was a veteran prospector and he was living on kangaroo meat at the time. He came to Rum Jungle looking for copper, but he had seen a government pamphlet describing the appearance of the new metal, uranium; and the ore he discovered in the old tin and copper workings seemed to him to bear a close resemblance to it. On 6 October 1949 he presented himself with a bag of samples at the Mines Department in Darwin. They were found to be strongly radio-active. Then the wet season closed down in November, and nothing could be done for the next few months. When the rains broke in the following March government experts were sent to Rum Jungle, and they carried out a series of geological surveys through 1950.

[1] This at any rate is the most widely accepted account of how the place got its name. There are other versions.

The results were all promising—the ore was rich and apparently boundless. Once more the Wet intervened, and then in March 1951 the workings began and the uranium boom was on. The government promised a reward of £1,000 for every new find, and an additional £1,000 up to a maximum of £25,000 for every twenty-five tons of ore got out of the ground.

White, of course, was the first man in the field. He sank an experimental shaft at Rum Jungle with such speed (using only a pick and shovel and a bucket attached to a windlass) that the retaining timbers came adrift above his head and he was nearly smothered by falling rock. But he found uranium all the way down, and he had his £25,000 clearly in view. Two larger shafts were then put in by the government with the same result, and diamond drilling was begun to determine the extent of the field. When I first saw Rum Jungle a year later, in the winter of 1952, it was an established mine.

There was no difficulty in reaching the place. We simply took a car in Darwin and drove down the Bitumen through arid broken hills until we reached the 54th milestone; then we turned west along a side road to a deserted landing field made by the air force in the war. Half a dozen miles further on along a gravelled track my guide stopped the car and announced that we were in Rum Jungle. It was, I must confess, a sad disappointment. Most of the ground was covered with monotonous gum-tree scrub, though there *was* a jungle of sorts close by—a line of green mangoes and other tropical plants covering an area not much bigger than the greenhouses in Kew Gardens. Somewhere in the undergrowth presumably was the famous rum waterpool. A lonely narrow-gauge railway meandered through the scrub, and Rum Jungle station was nothing more than a siding with a couple of trucks waiting there; no building of any kind.

The miners' camp lay a little above the railway on a flat

hilltop and about half a mile away. It looked like one of those coloured prints of the early Australian gold diggings. The largest building was the miners' mess, a rectangular iron shed which had once been used as an army detention barracks in the war; crossed bars and barbed wire were still fixed to the windows. In front of this was a dusty open compound on which the miners had put up their tents. Each tent had a canvas roof and a skirting of corrugated iron, which was designed to keep out the worst of the tropical rain during the Wet. Some of the men had relieved the uninspiring scene by growing bananas outside their tents; in this climate the trees bear fruit within nine months of being planted.

I was given a gargantuan but rumless meal in the detention barracks (a normal breakfast in the north consists of a pound or two of steak with two fried eggs on the top), and then we went off to see the mines. Uranium mines are, apparently, no different from any other in their outward appearance, at any rate in their early stages. There was a tangle of tramway lines with their squat triangular trucks, iron sheds with the power plants inside, long heaps of dark-grey rock brought up from the mine, and the usual gibbet-like structure of wooden beams over the shafts. The miners went down in a bucket suspended on the end of a steel rope, and that same bucket brought the ore to the top, where it was tipped into metal drums ready to be sent away. At that time the shafts were so shallow that you could see the bottom from the surface.

Uranium lay all about us at our feet. At Rum Jungle it is found in a soft slate which is easy to work, and it is colourless in its natural state in the ground. But once exposed to the air it oxidizes and shows up either as emerald green or a bright canary yellow in the slate. Although there is not enough uranium in this crude state to do any harm, you cannot avoid a slightly uneasy feeling when you first come to Rum Jungle, and see so much of it lying around. Most of the miners work in boots and shorts and nothing else, and indeed, even on this midwinter day it was hot.

The Australian bush is a mighty debunker of theatrical ideas. It is so silent, so incredibly old. An infinity of unexciting time presses around you as you walk through that interminable dry scrub. At Rum Jungle they had made as yet only a slight impression on the enormous silence, and the place might have been very dismal indeed except that there was a certain buoyancy in the miners themselves. They carried about with them an atmosphere such as you sense in a casino after someone has had a big win: the feeling that wealth is just around the corner, a thing of chance, and if someone else can touch it why not you? I called on Jack White—he lived in a slightly more elaborate tent a little apart from the others—but found him out. He had gone off with a geiger counter looking for other Rum Jungles in the bush. It was a spirit of which my Uncle Bill would have strongly approved.

It was, of course, an incredible piece of luck that Rum Jungle should lie just where it does, alongside a road and a railway, with an airfield and a supply of water close by, and a deep-sea port at Darwin only an hour away. These things have saved the Australian government many millions of pounds, for the field might just as easily have been found hundreds of miles away in the inaccessible desert. It was also good luck that there should be such an imperative demand for uranium in the world, and no signs of that demand ever diminishing. Under a contract made with the Joint Agency for Atomic Energy in the United States (the agency which is handling the supplies of uranium in the Western world), the Rum Jungle ore is being exported to America for processing until Australia builds plants and atomic piles of her own.

What was not so fortunate, however, was that carefree deal made with the absent landlords in the eighteen-sixties.

Most of the original owners are now dead, but their descendants and their heirs survive, and lately they have been evincing a very keen interest in their property. Were not all mining rights granted to the owners? Hardly a week goes by in the Lands Department in Darwin without some new claimant turning up. Old ladies, now living by the seaside in England, remember that Great Uncle Charles (regarded as rather a black sheep at the time) went off to Australia in the 'sixties, and did he not leave them a block of land, up there in the north somewhere? The north is as big as half Europe, but old ladies in Eastbourne and Brighton are not always aware of this, and anyway it's worth sending a letter to inquire. All sorts of documents are coming to light from family archives and solicitors' files: title deeds that were never worth anything until this moment, vague maps with vague markings, casual descriptions of hillsides that were won in a bet or lost in a bankruptcy court. Only the aborigines, who presumably are the real owners of the land, appear to have made no claim at all.

The whole issue is further bedevilled by the fact that the Rum Jungle land was never properly surveyed in the first place; in the 'sixties half a mile either way hardly made much difference. It was all part of the endless bush and quite useless.

Faced with these difficulties the Australian government has taken what is probably the only possible course. A Bill has been enacted making all uranium government property; and it has been announced that some compensation is to be made to the proven owners of the land, not enough to make their fortunes, but at any rate some reasonable sum.

No one pretends that Rum Jungle is, overnight, going to reverse the fortunes of the north, but it does at least hold out the prospect that a new California will be created here on the Arafura Sea, and that Stuart's dreams of a century ago will be justified at last. Indeed, I know of only one other place in Australia where there is such a tangible feeling of the future, and I must mention it here because it is part of the Stuart story, and it has its place in this sudden awakening of the north. This is the rocket range at Woomera, 1,200 miles to the south. Stuart passed by the place and ignored it on several of his journeys, for it is one of the most desolate areas of the interior. It has just one advantage: uninhabited space, and that was precisely what the scientists needed for their experiments with rockets and guided missiles after the last world war.

Woomera is no more than a dot on the empty map three hundred miles to the north-west of Adelaide. A long pipe-line brings water across the desert, and there is an hermetic little township of wooden and aluminium prefabricated houses, cut off from all the world except those who arrive by plane with special passes. The range itself is vast. It stretches for twelve hundred miles across the Great Sandy Desert to the north-west coastline of Australia. There-after, if the scientists want still more space, they can send their missiles flying on for another thousand miles past Monte Bello Island (where the first British atomic bomb was exploded in 1952) to Christmas Island in the Indian Ocean.

This region really is a desolation. The waterless plain stretches away apparently into infinity, with just an occasional line of parched trees and salt bush dotted about over the grey-brown earth. The atmosphere is almost ideal for the use of rockets. In that clear air the stars shine out like lanterns, and a tree or a cairn of stones which you imagine to be only a mile or two away is, in fact, divided from you by a dozen miles or more. When you have been at Woomera for a few hours you find yourself looking up into the heavens, the mind leaps outward, and presently any extension of the imagination becomes a reasonable possibility.

The uneasy thing about places like Woomera and Rum

Jungle, of course, is that they have no real history, and no traditions behind them. They spring out of nothingness and their potential power is enormous. Until a year or two ago absolutely nothing had happened in this desert except the roamings of the aborigines and the kangaroos and the interminable munchings of the white ants. If there is any history at all behind Woomera it is of the slightest kind, and probably concerns Captain James Cook as much as anybody else. When he made his remarkable voyage to the South Seas in 1768 his first object, like the objects of the scientists at Woomera, lay not upon this earth but in the heavens. He was instructed to observe the transit of Venus from the island of Tahiti. Then, almost as an afterthought, he was ordered to discover 'whether the unexplored part of the southern hemisphere be only an immense mass of water or contain another continent'.

On 3 June 1769, Venus was successfully observed, and Cook then sailed on to explore the eastern seaboard of Australia. It was at his very first contact with the aborigines at Botany Bay that he saw them handling a curious weapon, called a woomera. It consisted of a long hollowed-out piece of wood, and its shape was not unlike that of the basket which the Basques strap to their wrists when they play the game of pelota. There was a notch at the end of the woomera to which the spear was fitted, and the purpose of the whole contraption was to give extra leverage and to guide the spear upon its way. The spear, in fact, was a guided missile, and from this weapon the rocket range has taken its name.

The launching ramps for the rockets lie some little distance from the township of Woomera, and they point up silently into the sky like signposts. For the most part they are simple trestles of steel bedded in concrete, and the runway for the rocket slopes sharply upward. The rocket, a long, thin, pencil-shaped affair with a pointed nose and steel fins, goes off with a tremendous roar, belching flame and smoke behind it. Just for an instant the human eye holds it in view until it vanishes, at supersonic speed, into realms where only pure mathematics can follow. And what makes it all so odd is that, all around you on the benighted plain, the antediluvian animals of Australia sit quietly watching. It is this conjunction of the infinitely primitive past and the infinitely fantastic future that makes Woomera so strange and stimulating a place.

One looks at the bright little township, the workshops, the calculating machines, the cameras, the pilotless plane, and the rocket, and the net result of it all is to reduce you to the status of an ant. Perhaps even less than an ant, for if you like to overturn one of the myriad anthills round about you will discover a precise and ordered life going on there, an abysmal life perhaps, but quite as marvellous as anything that human beings have achieved as yet, since they have the secret of the predetermination of sex, and they know the means of procreating and protecting the race in perfect security.

There is no security in what human beings are doing at Woomera, only more insecurity. The scientists go on experimenting in an incalculable void. Either death or Nirvana lie ahead; either we will reach the moon or end up by burrowing underground for self-protection like the ants —but we must go on.

I suppose the place is fixed with such a sense of unreality in my mind because I was only there for a day. I set out from Adelaide in the very early morning. It was cold and wet, and at the airfield where the transcontinental planes kept lighting down in the darkness one was surrounded by the strained and exhausted faces of people who had been travelling all night. A loudspeaker kept barking at them and they moved obediently like sheep. When my own plane took off it was still dark and still raining; and since we were bound only for the desert the illusion of unreality was compelling. We sat there for a long time

in that cold metal box in the sky—how horrible is any
early morning journey in the air however often you repeat
it—until the sun came up reluctantly through the rain
clouds at the tip of Spenser's Gulf. Then we flew on into
the emptiness of the north.

After so dismal a flight I found Woomera itself posi-
tively gay. The sun shone out, the air was warm, and two
kangaroos went bounding away from under the wings of
the plane as we landed. But all the rest of the things they
showed me that day belonged to another world. We drove
for five or six hours along old cattle trails that led from
one waterhole to the next. Most of the time there was
nothing to see except more barren space opening up
before us. Then for no apparent reason a shed or an out-
building of some kind would pop up on the horizon. It
looked like any other bush shanty from the distance, but
when one drew near one found it humming with electrical
machinery, and men were working there at instruments
that looked like giant adding machines, full of complicated
wires and flickering lights. Mugs of tea stood on an upturned wooden box in the corner, a cat nestled on a pile
of month-old magazines and newspapers, and outside there
was nothing but the wilderness.

One can understand in a general way the object of these
experiments: the war of the rockets and atomic explosions
in the fathomless sky. But I doubt if I comprehended the
gadgets at Woomera any better than the wedge-tailed
eagles flying overhead, or the wallaby that sat, just a few
yards away, gravely regarding us across the sand. Always
those animals and the antiseptic timelessness of the desert.

There was just one moment towards evening when I
did understand at any rate the spirit of the place. A moon
came up, clearer and brighter almost than any new moon I
had ever seen before. While it was still pale silver and
there was still half an hour left of that marvellous slanting
sunset light, my guide, a group captain in the Australian

Air Force, drove me to a place called Lake Hart. Normally, like most of the central Australian lakes, it is quite dry: a simple expanse of white salt with high cliffs jutting up around it; but recently there had been rain, and the salt had turned to a shade of burnt sienna. We got out of the car and stood on the rocky crest of the cliff. The visibility was quite extraordinary: I saw a clump of trees at the opposite end of the lake and that was nearly twenty miles away. There had been bombing tests along the lake— ordinary mundane bombs—and they had made a pattern of star-like craters on the dark surface of the mud. There was no wind and no sound anywhere. A superb eagle kept circling across the face of the red cliff, apparently on the lookout for rabbits or some other game on the ground. Three kangaroos were grazing quietly in the tussocks of grass behind us. They were nervous at first, and kept sitting back on their tails so that they could get a better view of the two of us, standing there on the cliff-top; but presently they were reassured and dropped their heads meekly to the grass again. 'It's a pretty place,' the Group Captain was saying, and we glanced up to the moon together, now that it was bright golden-yellow and the best of the sunset colours had gone from the air. It had been a day of brassy sunshine, and now the sky had turned to a shade of velvet indigo, and seemed to be drawing much nearer to the earth. The stars were quite incredibly bright. We looked up past the moon and the Southern Cross to the continuous white path of the Milky Way. We had had such a day among the launching ramps and the rockets that it was not difficult to know what the Group Captain was thinking. The moon—it was not so far away. And if you could reach the moon why not all the rest?—Jupiter and Mars and Venus herself, riding up there somewhere, as Captain Cook had noted, upon a predictable speed and course.

It was beginning to turn a little cold. As we got back

into the car, the three kangaroos reared up from the grass
and with a long swinging motion went bounding off
somewhere into the darkness.

Between the rockets and the atomic power, between
those holes in the ground at Rum Jungle and these horizons
at Woomera, what a fantasy lies ahead of this empty
country. No wonder that, despite all the mismanagement,
the work and the certain tragedy that lies ahead, there is
an undercurrent excitement in the north, a sense of life
to be. On my journeys I met just one man who seemed to
be apart from it all. He was a Czechoslovakian geologist
at Rum Jungle, and he had lately arrived in Australia from
behind the Iron Curtain. Life had not been very gay in
Prague since the communist *coup d'état*. Now he sat under
a banana tree reading the *Journals* of André Gide. 'I like
it here,' he said. 'Most Europeans say they get restless in
the Australian bush, but for me it has everything I want—
I can have music, books, and all this. . . .' He waved his
hand towards the jungle and the sulphur-crested cockatoos.
'I have seen enough of the other sort of world in Europe.
Here you can have a simple life.'

But his chances of enjoying the simple life at Rum Jungle
did not seem very good. There was a bulldozer at work
among the mangoes and the bamboos. Workmen were
putting up the first of the new houses for the miners. It
did not take much imagination to foresee a city here, complete with air-conditioned buildings, a security guard, a
roaring airfield, an atomic pile, and all the other wonderful
things that lie in the white man's dreaming.

CHAPTER SEVEN

Demoiselles and Bullseyes

ANYONE exploring Northern Australia must, if he is wise, turn eastwards at some point and see the Great Barrier Reef. It is an immense agglomeration of coral, the largest that exists. It runs for 1,250 miles along the north-eastern seaboard of the continent, almost from the Equator to the Tropic of Capricorn, and covers an area of some 80,000 square miles.

There is no one continuous wall of coral. It consists, instead, of thousands of small reefs which run in all direc-tions beneath the sea and sprout up to the surface like the hedges of an informal garden. Some of them are a few yards wide, others a quarter of a mile or more, and lagoons of relatively shallow water lie in between.

When you go out to the Reef from the mainland (it is usually a journey of several hours), your pilot has to pick his way very carefully between the different shoals, until at last, far out of sight of the coast, he reaches the final shoal which is known as the Outer Reef; and here the coral plunges steeply down, like the face of a precipice, into the depths of the Pacific.

The usual thing is to take a launch out from one of the North Queensland coastal towns, and on arriving at the Reef you transfer into a smaller boat with a glass bottom, so that you can peer down at the coral a foot or two below. At low tide you can get out of these boats and walk along on the coral itself.

On my first trip we set out from Townsville in a small boat called the *Paluma* at seven-thirty in the morning. We

103

were a small party consisting mostly of fanatical deep-sea
fishermen and a few other tourists like myself. We sailed
directly into the winter sun, and it was a perfect day: perfect, that is, for the first hour and to all outward appear-
ances.

After we cleared Magnetic Island, the nearest and the
largest of the islands off the mainland, the sun still shone
but a ferocious wind drove across the surface of the sea,
and there was never an instant when you could stand on
the *Paluma's* wet decks without holding on with both
hands. This went on for three hours while the mainland
vanished over the horizon. I don't think I can remember
any trip quite so rough as this. One woman lay upon a bunk
panting in misery throughout the entire journey, and there
were moments when the captain contemplated turning
back. But the deep-sea fishermen were having a wonderful
time hauling in four-foot Spanish mackerel from long lines
over the stern, and the rest of us were too caught up with
the scene around us to give way to sea-sickness; so we
went on.

Just at that time of the year—it was July—the whales
come back from the Antarctic, and we could see them
moving about in the distance. Later, on other trips, I was
to get to know the whales much better and from much
nearer at hand, but it's the first sight of a whale from a
small boat that really takes you aback. No matter what
you have heard or read about whales, they still seem quite
monstrously and impossibly large when you see them like
this, swimming about in the sea. You notice them first,
from a long way off, spouting on the horizon. Then, as
they come cruising nearer to investigate your boat, you
see that they are playing like dolphins, often in groups of
two or three, but with a cumbersome frolicsome motion
that never seems to be entirely under control. As they
break the surface the water comes streaming off their
backs in a waterfall. You get a brief glimpse of a round

and merry eye, and then they dive, flicking up their tails behind them into the sky. They never attack small boats, though occasionally they try to rub the barnacles off their backs along the keel. Still, it's quite frightening to see them from a hundred yards away; you have a feeling of fatalistic helplessness, and when the captain of the *Paluma* told me that they roar in the depths at night with a horrible and awe-inspiring sound I found I could well believe him.

After the whales everything at sea tends to be rather an anticlimax, but I thought the small fish on this trip immensely entertaining. They appeared in tens of thousands, apparently driven up to the surface by some monster lurking on the ocean floor. For a moment all the warm surface of the water became ruffled as though a sudden wind had swept across it. Then the fish sailed clear into the air in a continuous silver stream and flopped back again with a patter like falling rain. There was a convoy of gulls and other sea birds following in the wake of our boat, and this was the moment they had been waiting for. They plummeted down with their beaks wide open, and landed with an explosive 'plop' in the sea. Then they took off again, gobbling fish as they flew.

It was around midday when we sighted the Outer Reef. At first I could see nothing but a long navy-blue wall stretching across the horizon, and the top of this wall was flecked with white. It looked as though a tidal wave was travelling across the sea towards us. This, the captain, explained, was the long swell of the Pacific breaking on the outer edge of the coral. Then, as we drew nearer, we could see the shallow lagoons on the lee side, and in the midst of the dark surrounding ocean these lagoons looked as though they had been stained by some chemical into the airiest and most transparent of colours: very pale blues and yellowish greens. There were no waves in the lagoons and presently the *Paluma* sailed into that blessed calm in the middle of the ocean and anchored there. All around us

"Some of the coral reaches up towards you in a forest of antlers."

Australian National Publicity Association

A section of the reef exposed at low tide among the islands

were the 'niggerheads' sticking out of the water: large
chunks of coral that had been broken off in a storm and
tossed on top of the living reef. Down below us—and the
water was transparent enough to allow one to see down
for fifty feet or more—were the coral, the seaweeds, and
the fish.

While the fishermen hauled in their lines and someone
revived the seasick lady on her bunk, a rowing boat was
put out from the *Paluma* and half a dozen of us scrambled
into it. A sort of glass box was built into the floor of the
boat, and we crouched around this looking down at the
coral in much the same way as you would look into a
television screen. For the next hour we were gently rowed
about while we simply sat there, looking downwards.

Nothing in one's past experience can quite prepare you
for the first sight of the coral. Afterwards it remains
startlingly bright in the memory, it fills the mind's eye
with all the original movement and colour; and one enjoys
again, after so much adult disbelief, the simple feeling of
wonder. Perhaps the only comparable thing is that moment
when, as a child, one was taken to a theatre and saw for
the first time the curtain going up on the bright lights and
the actors on the stage.

Some of the coral reaches up towards you in a forest of
antlers, coloured heliotrope, or pink, or cobalt, or saffron
yellow. But it takes many other forms as well; sometimes
it looks like trees in blossom, or it runs in ridges like the
underside of a mushroom, or it is lumped and pitted like
the cells of a human brain. There are great flat-tops in the
shape of water-lilies, beehive formations, blocks of honey-
comb, and here and there a kind of moss, like a penicillin
culture. When the coral is feeding its extended tendrils
undulate and wave about in the current with the trailing
motion of ferns in a breeze.

In the Reef there are many great gulches and caverns
sprouting with life all the way down, until on the clear

bottom you see repulsive fat slugs, a foot or more in length, called bêches-de-mer; and giant clams, the size of an office desk. These clams have their jaws gaping open, and all the interior is lined with a velvety mass of flesh, coloured emerald green or indigo or scarlet. It is said that a giant clam will seize a diver by the leg and hold him till he drowns. All the people who really know the Reef deny this story, yet, as you look down into those gaping jaws you can see how it *might* happen; and you shudder.

Through this garden the fish are constantly swimming: the Red Emperors in a kind of stage version of the robes of Japanese mikados, the coral trout dotted with blue spots, the Parrot Fish in the hues of a rainbow, the Harlequin Smiler and the Butterfly Cod, many of them weighing up to twenty pounds and more. I saw two smaller species of a strange luminous colour, one of them a nervous little fish about an inch long and shaded a bright electric blue, and the other boldly marked in yellow and black stripes; and I asked the boatman what they were. 'Those,' he said, 'are Demoiselles and Bullseyes.'

I had only an hour or so on the Reef on this first visit before we sailed back to Townsville, but it was enough to make me decide to scrap all other plans and spend the next few weeks on the coast. Above all I wanted to get out and walk on the Reef itself during a really low tide; and for that I had to wait ten days. I stayed in one of the island hotels south of Townsville, and then towards the middle of July set out for the Outer Reef again. This time it was a smaller boat than the *Paluma* but the sea was calmer.

Again we saw that wall of water across the horizon, but there was something added; slowly and mysteriously the coral itself emerged from the sea. As the tide ebbed away the niggerheads came fully into view like so many giant mushrooms, and then we found ourselves sailing along the edge of a low platform of coral. I imagine that in Arctic waters one comes up to the ice floe in just this

Australian National Publicity Association

Butterfly cod cruising through a rock pool in the Reef

way. The particular reef we were making for was not very
wide—a quarter of a mile or so—but it stretched away on
either side of us as far as we could see. From the distance
its surface appeared to be quite flat, and the general colour
of the coral was a disappointing oyster-grey. It was only
when we came ashore and walked on the reef—and it is
just as well to wear a pair of heavy tennis shoes—that we
discovered that, from close at hand, it has the colours of a
patchwork quilt; and all of it is alive. In the shallow pools
left behind by the receding tide a tremendous activity goes
on. Sea-snakes glide among the reeds and the shells. The
crabs, a special species of coral crab with one great claw
always stretched towards the point of danger, have a quick
and darting movement unlike anything in an aquarium,
and the anemones cringe with a sudden furtive contrac-
tion when they are touched. As you walk along the clams
shut tight their velvet mouths and send up little geysers
all around you.

While on the Reef you are always conscious of the
ominous sea breaking on the outer edge, and of that
mighty precipice reaching down into the Pacific. But you
splash on from pool to pool in a kind of trance, slipping on
patches of slimy seaweed, stopping to chase the fish or
gather shells and starfish, and always wanting to look at
just one more pool ahead.

After an hour or more of this you begin to notice that
you are no longer walking on dry coral; the warm salt
water is washing round your ankles. Then you look up and
see how far you have wandered; and this is a moment of
fear. All the rest of the reef has vanished in the rising tide,
and there is nothing but the sea around you. Except for
your boat, a small toy away in the distance, you are alone
in the middle of the Pacific, with the tide still coming in,
and along with the tide the sharks.

Then you bolt for your boat. You may have plenty of
time, half an hour or more, before the water will be up to

your waist, which is about as high as it rises, but you don't know this, and you slip and slither over the uncertain ground until you get back to your friends and, with a rather hollow show of nonchalance, scramble on board.

There is, in fact, always this quality of menace about the Reef, and you feel it very strongly when you are there. It is never at peace. Everything that lives on it is engaged in a pitiless struggle for existence, and often the most beautiful things are the most murderous. Even at its quietest moments there is, as in the landscapes of the Douanier Rousseau, always some monster lurking in the background and ready to spring. I made a number of trips out to the Reef at high and low water, and although I was always fascinated I never felt completely at ease.

Often as you are gazing through the glass bottom of your boat (and this was something which I found I could do for days on end), you will see an idyllic scene. The Red Emperors, the Demoiselles, and the Bullseyes drift about, the living coral waves idly, and even the crabs are at rest. Then suddenly, as though some trumpet call had sounded in the water, the fish vanish and every living thing lies perfectly still. You wait and watch. And then presently the rounded nose of a grey nurse shark comes cruising into your line of vision, the most murderous brute of all, who will kill, it seems, out of a straight lust for blood. Quite a long time elapses after the shark has gone before the fish emerge and the normal life of the sea takes up its course again.

Then there are lovely cone-shaped sea shells marked with a geometrical pattern of brown diamonds, not unlike a batik cloth. A dangerous crab-like animal lurks inside. If you reach down to pick one up it darts out a sting which is so poisonous that people have been killed by the first shock of unbearable pain. You lose your senses one by one, becoming first deaf, then blind, until finally all your body is paralysed, and the agony is such that you have no will to cry out or move in any way. Death sometimes follows in an hour or even less. The usual treatment now is to inject morphia, which enables the patient to bear the pain while his body adjusts itself to the poison.

The stone-fish has this same evil power, but with the fish its very appearance is a warning. It must be the ugliest creature in existence, a slimy discoloured fiend with a glaring eye and a skin covered in warts. It lies motionless in the shallow pools of the reef, and there are thirteen quills on its back, each loaded with poison. If you step with a bare foot on these quills the same paralysis sets in at once, and even if you survive the first shock the agony will come back again and again in after weeks like recurring bouts of malaria.

There is another sort of drama which goes on just at dusk each evening, and which seemed to me to be almost as ruthless in its way as anything conjured up by the stone-fish or the shark. If you look upwards in the failing light you will often see, far up in the sky, a tiny dark speck. This is the frigate-bird. He is a mighty flyer, and he stays poised up there, quite motionless, with his head against the wind. Then he dives, and it is a power-dive of tremendous speed. His quarry, usually, is a seagull flying home with a crop full of fish to feed its young.

The gull sights the frigate-bird tearing down on him and he panics at once: he disgorges the fish in order to get away. Then the frigate-bird dives below the gull and snatches up the falling fish in mid-air. Half a dozen such dives can produce quite an acceptable meal for the frigate-bird, after which presumably he goes off home to feed *his* young. One might have a good deal more pity for the gulls if one did not know that they prey upon the lesser birds like the terns in exactly the same way; and the terns themselves have another sort of piracy of their own. Indeed everything above, below, or on the Reef is eating or being eaten, destroying or being destroyed. This is the overmastering rule, and only the shark appears to be exempt from it. After you have been on the Reef for a while you begin to feel that, by comparison, human affairs are mild almost to the point of senility. There could scarcely be a man-made war quite so horrible as the things that go on night after night in this over-populated sea.

Captain James Cook, the navigator, was probably the first white man to see the Reef when he arrived off the Australian coast in 1770 in his ship *The Endeavour*; and for him the Reef was not a beautiful thing but a horror. *The Endeavour* was badly holed on the coral, and when he first caught sight of the splendid vision of the sea breaking on the Outer Reef he described it simply as 'a dreadful surf'. Certainly if Captain Cook had had any notion of the size and complexity of these coral shoals he would have been more alarmed than he was, for no one has succeeded in charting them fully, even yet.

The polyp, the animal which has created this extraordinary submarine empire, is a relatively simple organism about the size of a pinhead. It lives in colonies, is fixed to a hard shell which it secretes about itself, and it feeds by shooting out venomous tendrils at such minute creatures of the sea as happen to be passing by. It has, however, in certain circumstances, one engaging attribute; it can change its sex at will, and it can also be an hermaphrodite. Just how or why this ambidexterity should happen is not altogether clear (does a polyp catch sight of another good-looking male and instantly turn himself into a female?), but at least it is certain that this tiny creature is as ageless as the sea and immensely prolific. It needs, of course, tropical or semi-tropical water. When it is exposed to the air for more than a few hours it dies; if you snap off a branch it soon loses its brilliant delicate colour and turns to a dirty grey. It cannot live at greater depths than a hundred and fifty feet, and it is for this reason that only the top of the Reef is alive. All the rest, the immense wall

"Such myriads that you can scarcely avoid stepping on them

you come ashore.'' Terns on a Barrier Reef Island

that reaches down for miles into the sea, is simply a heap of dead bones, the skeletons of innumerable generations of coral polyps and the debris of the ocean floor. Sometimes when you look down through the glass bottom of your boat you can see this very clearly—the vast charnel house of dead and broken branches plunging into the black abyss of water, but always with the living glowing coral rising on the top, close to the surface of the sea.

Naturally this phenomenon aroused a great deal of interest in the early days of marine exploration. If the polyp died at greater depths than a hundred and fifty feet, how did it ever construct these huge walls so deep in the Pacific? The coral below there in the depths must have been alive at some time.

It was left to Charles Darwin to provide a convincing answer. Darwin, then a young man of twenty-seven, turned up in the Pacific sixty-one years after Cook, when he was attached to a British scientific expedition aboard Her Majesty's ship *Beagle*. He made a study of the coral. On his return to England he issued a paper in which he announced that the floor of the Pacific must have been sinking through past geological ages. As the seabed went down the coral polyp kept building upwards on his dead self to the warmth and light of the surface water.

Among geologists this idea caused almost as much disturbance as Darwin's views on the origin of the human species which he published later on; but his theory is generally accepted now. It got strong support again in 1946 when scientists went out to Bikini Island before the atomic bomb was exploded there. Five bores were sunk through the coral to a depth of 2,556 feet, and seismic soundings went even deeper before they struck the basic rock of the sea bed. These experiments established that the coral at Bikini went down to a depth of about seven thousand feet, and that some of it must have been formed twenty to thirty million years ago in the Miocene Age.

Certainly the existence of those islands between the Reef
and the mainland, which are simply sunken mountain tops,
would seem to prove Darwin's theory: and there is ample
evidence to show that the Pacific has not found its permanent level even yet. However, there are no signs of the
polyp being defeated. Storms bash the reefs about at times,
and drive holes in them, but such things are only slight
interruptions in a vast communal life that counts time not
by years or centuries, but by millenniums.

After you have seen the Reef itself the thing to do is to
explore the islands, or at any rate some of them, for there
are about six hundred in all. The smaller and flatter ones
are known as 'cays', and these lie on the top of the coral.
For the most part they are only an acre or two in extent;
and they have been formed by driftwood and ocean debris
gradually collecting together through the centuries and
making a kind of soil on top of the Reef. There is usually
vegetation of some kind—the droppings of the seabirds
contain seeds that spring up later into tropical undergrowth.

The larger islands are the sunken mountain tops, and
they lie close to the coast line. Very few of them are in-
habited. Natives from the South Pacific tribes may have
lived on them once, but now the uncut virgin jungle rises
up from the water's edge, and if you except the teeming
birds, the turtles, and the lizards, there is no life on them.
Just occasionally, as you sail by, you may catch a glimpse
of something white moving among the coconut palms.
These are the goats which the Australian government set
up on the islands many years ago, so that shipwrecked
mariners could sustain life if they were washed ashore.
Nowadays the goats are so wild that a mariner would have
to be a very spry fellow indeed to succeed in catching one.
When wrecks occur on the coral, as they still do, the
survivors try and make for the mainland.

I landed at half a dozen of these islands, some of them

Heron Island, a coral bay, formed by driftwood and ocean debris gathering on top of the Reef. The dark patches in the foreground are the coral growing beneath the surface of the sea

barely large enough to have a name, and found that nearly all of them are surrounded by coral, so that your boat has to steer a careful course towards the beach. Then you step straight ashore into the cool green tropical undergrowth. It is this juxtaposition of the jungle and the coral—the green gloom of the creepers and the trees above and the bright life of the coral depths below—that gives these places a wonderful storybook quality.

There is too an indescribable satisfaction in setting your foot down on ground where probably no one else has ever been before. You feel that the sea, the Reef, and the jungle are entirely powerful, and that you yourself are only a midget on the scene. Still, here you are, as lonely and as indomitable as Robinson Crusoe, and all that happens here is for your eyes alone.

Possibly this is the real charm of the islands. That slightly enervating air which one can only describe as a tourist staleness has not yet descended on them. Unlike the Grand Canyon or the Egyptian Pyramids or most of the other wonders of the world, these places have not been wondered at, looked at, thought about, painted, photographed, or described to any great extent; and so one arrives without any preconceived picture in the mind. It's all yours, to be explored in your own good time. Here on the beach you can see the footprints made by the green turtles as they wade ashore to lay their eggs in a hole in the sand; and you know that when the eggs hatch the baby turtles will fumble their way down to the water's edge where the sharks are waiting. You can observe, if you wish, a certain jet-propelled scallop that moves along by taking in water at one end and disgorging it out the other.

The bright red and blue starfish in the pools, the cowrie shells, the oysters that you eat alive from the rocks, the sinister orchids on the trees, and the diving frigate-bird are all your personal discoveries. When someone tells you that there exists a certain fish that climbs trees you can, with persistence, find a specimen actually perching there before you; and there are vales filled with tropical butterflies where no one but you has been before.

Better still, you can see a mermaid, or at any rate the animal that spread the legend in the Pacific. This is the dugong. It has a large shapeless body weighing perhaps half a ton, and its face is a comic and unlovely thing. In the cold light of day there is no agility of the imagination which could transform the dugong into a mermaid. But when one rises glistening in the moonlight and floats on the surface of the sea—especially a female clutching a baby with one flipper to its breast—it is not hard to understand how the love-lorn sailors began to dream dreams which are as old as Ulysses and the sirens. The scientific name for the order of dugongs is, in fact, *Sirenia*. The Australians call it a sea-cow.

Each island you visit seems to have some curiosity or monstrosity which is peculiarly its own. On Green Island there are rats living in the palms, apparently brought there by soldiers who landed in barges during the war. On Hinchinbrook Island there are supposed to be tree-pythons twenty feet in length. On Magnetic Island, which is only a few miles across the sea from Townsville, the pineapples, the pawpaws, and the flowering shrubs like the crotons and the poinsianas grow with a special abundance. Close by, on the mainland, there is a place called Alligator Creek, where a fish called the Yankee Whiting appears in millions for a few months every year, and only at this place. One of the Townsville fishermen and I took a boat out there one Sunday morning and we caught sixty fish in precisely sixty minutes. And that too is the place to watch the pelicans. As they come in for a landing they have an absurd way of putting out their webbed feet before them like buffers, so that the water streams out in a long wake in their rear. On Hayman Island the Kurrawong bird calls endlessly all day with a cry exactly like its name, and on

Pandanus palms, sometimes known as "walking trees." Yo

nd them on nearly all the islands

North-west Island the mutton-birds arrive in such myriads that you can scarcely avoid stepping on them as you come ashore.

After a time, as you travel back and forth between the mainland and the islands, you are prepared to accept any oddity: foxes that fly through the trees, hordes of crabs that march by night across the beach in military formation, octopuses that burrow in sand, and green ants that stitch their leaf-houses together by holding their babies in their arms and drawing out of the babies' mouths a sticky thread as strong as cotton. I baulked at first at the stories of a certain frog called a Bufo which attacks chickens and makes a noise like a motor-cycle. But then one night in Townsville the people with whom I was dining brought one in from their garden, a monster half the size of a cat. It was imported from Honolulu, they said, to defeat the sugar-cane beetle.

In the end, probably it is the jungle that makes everything plausible. One can understand trees, however exotic they may be, and when you see them growing on these islands, from the very edge of the coral, they create a kind of reassurance in the mind; they make a guarantee that all the rest is real.

I used to love driving along the remote side-roads on the coast where the jungle was really thick. Even at midday no sunshine gets through to the ground; instead there is a cool green light such as you see in a darkened room when the shutters are closed on a midsummer day. Above your head the immense trees are laced together with vines and creepers that look like the rigging of a sailing ship. There is no sign of life anywhere, and the river pools are as still and dark as Indian ink.

Just how much longer these splendid jungles will continue is anybody's guess, for they are being gradually cleared away to make room for plantations of sugar-cane and tropical fruit. It is rather a shock sometimes to see what has already been done. I remember one day coming out of the jungle into a clearing just south of Cairns. You might have fancied that a typhoon had passed by. For twenty acres the trees had been clawed and hacked away, and in their place were neat lines of pineapples and bananas. They grew right to the edge of the clearing, and beyond that the jungle rose up, a hundred feet or more into the air, and all the exposed face of it was savaged and scarred as though some huge claw had been tearing at it. This was the work of just one farmer. ·

He stood there, this one small man, surrounded by the wreckage. Trees with trunks as thick as bandstands soared up above us with ferns sprouting out of their branches, and they had been growing quietly there in the tropical rain since beyond the days of Queen Victoria and Napoleon. But they came down very quickly. As we were talking, one of the farmer's sons called to us from somewhere in the green shadows to stand back; and then a giant fig came hurtling down with a gargantuan crash through the branches of the other trees, trailing its vines and creepers behind it.

One of his troubles, the farmer explained, was that as soon as these big trees were cut down and sunlight hit the ground for the first time, a forest of tropical shrubs rushed in and took possession of the clean soil; this too had to be hacked away.

Since the war a number of these fishermen-farmers are setting themselves up, and it is clear that a good deal of the present wild beauty of the country is going to vanish in the process of making it truly civilized. The extraordinary thing, of course, is that not more people have discovered this coast. For a thousand miles, from the town of Rockhampton on the Tropic of Capricorn to the tip of Cape York peninsula, it is certainly as beautiful as anything on the Mediterranean, as productive as California. Yet there are hardly more than a hundred thousand inhabitants, and most of these are grouped in the three chief towns of Townsville, Cairns, and Mackay.

Townsville is an attractive place, just north of the twentieth parallel, and with 40,000 inhabitants it claims to have the largest white population of any tropical town in the world. Green lawns dotted with palms run down to the water's edge, and all the sea horizon is broken by the crests of wild islands. A bluff of rock called Castle Hill rises sheer for a thousand feet behind the town, and if you climb up there at night to look down on the traffic and the lights of the city you might well imagine you were in San Francisco.

Townsville is the port for the lead mines, and the big cattle and sheep properties in the interior. Another of its interests is catering for the tourists who arrive in winter from the colder states of the Commonwealth, a thousand miles and more to the south. There is a lively industry in selling bits of coral which, having died and faded in the air, have been repainted in bright but not very convincing colours. I noticed one souvenir shop where they had had the horrible idea of stuffing baby alligators and dressing them up like golfers with tartan caps and golf bags. There is, too, just outside the town a delightful native zoo, where ibis and storks pick their way in hundreds through the lilac and blood-red lilies in the lagoons. If there is a large enough crowd the keeper will box the kangaroo and prod the alligators so that they will make a whirring clockwork noise like some monstrous mechanical toy.

Cairns, the town further north, has one unique thing: an airfield that floats. It is built on mudflats by the sea, and the tarmac rises and falls slightly with the tide.

The American Army knew all this country very well in the last war; eighty thousand soldiers and airmen were hurriedly sent here after the fall of the Philippines, when it looked as if the Japanese were going to come on to Australia. The Americans are remembered now for their extraordinary celerity. They went up into the Atherton Tablelands—the massif that rises from the coast behind Cairns—and built camps almost overnight. When they had no bitumen with which to make airfields they took barrels of molasses from the sugar-cane factories and made runways out of that. With DDT they banished the mosquitoes (which have since returned), and they brought more life to Cairns and Townsville than the local people had seen in many a long day.

When at last the Japanese fleet was destroyed in the Battle of the Coral Sea, and the war moved north through New Guinea to the East Indies and Japan, the Americans vanished like Cambyses' army in the desert, and left nothing much behind except, on the whole, an agreeable and grateful reputation. It was hoped that after the war they would come back, and that tourists would flow in from all over the world. But somehow it hasn't happened. Like Stevenson's Treasure Island, the South Pacific remains more of a pleasant idea in people's minds than a place to visit; it looks romantic on the stage or in a book but it is hardly practical. It is too hot: too far away.

So the Reef and the coast remain pretty much as the soldiers saw them during the war. And yet, quite apart from the unspoiled scenery above and below the sea, this surely must be one of the finest holiday places in the world. You can be sure of getting fish on almost any day you like to take out a boat anywhere along the coast, and it might be anything from the twenty-pound Spanish mackerel and the Harlequin Smiler right up to the marlin and the sharks. I personally never caught anything really big, I spent most of my time simply gazing at the coral, but I *did* see the turtles come mooning across the water with their sad scaly faces, and once an alligator slid up to the surface and took something from my line just at the moment when I was hauling it in.

As for the Reef itself, it remains almost deserted, miles

and miles of it, an infinity of coral, too much of it really
to comprehend, but perhaps in its way the loveliest thing
on earth. Here and there a floating mine or a wreck may
have gouged out a tiny hole in the long line; but all the
rest has returned to the same desperate quietism it always
had. The birds and the beasts and the fish continue, in the
normal way, to destroy one another in peace.

CHAPTER EIGHT

On Beachcombing

INEVITABLY while you are travelling on this coast there comes a moment when you ask yourself, 'Why don't I stay? Why don't I live here?' It would be so cheap and easy to build a house, to get a boat of your own, and in very little time—perhaps six months or even less—it would be possible to grow all the fruit and vegetables you would ever need. There would be no problem of heating and clothing; the weather remains pleasantly and steadily warm throughout the year. Nearly all the more harassing difficulties of city life simply vanish here, and money ceases to be an object in itself. There is a cheap and excellent rum made from sugar-cane on the coast, tobacco grows almost anywhere, and for the rest of your entertainment there is the Reef and the sea. Here really you would cease to live life at second hand and begin to expand in a natural way.

Apparently it has been done and with entire success by a certain Liverpool journalist called E. J. Banfield. His doctor diagnosed an early death for him, so he came to the Barrier Reef hoping to find an agreeable place where he could spin out the last few months of his existence. He chose Dunk Island, just off the mainland, not far from Cairns. The place was known to the aborigines as Coonanglebah, but Captain Cook, a man with a practical mind, renamed it after George M. Dunk, Earl of Halifax, the First Lord of the Admiralty. Banfield lived on in this island for twenty-six years, and under the pseudonym of 'The Beachcomber' wrote a series of books in thankfulness and praise of life on the Barrier Reef, especially Dunk Island.

I went to Dunk Island and found it to be not quite the ideal island, since an hotel has been established there now, and Banfield's tomb under the palm trees is a little gloomy. Perhaps my feelings about the place were affected by the man in charge of my launch. He said he was having a dispute with the people on the island, and although he came on shore with me he hardly spoke during the whole time we were there. It created a slightly uneasy atmosphere. However, I learned something that interested me very much. Beyond Dunk Island there was another island, much wilder, smaller, and just as beautiful, and an old friend of mine was living there. Since it is only fair to respect his privacy I will call him Bassett, which is not his real name, and his island Richards Island, which is not the name that appears on the maps. Bassett and I had been undergraduates together at the Melbourne University, and it seemed to be understood then that he was to go into one of the professions in the city.

I could not remember that he was odd in any way; he was rather an amiable and gregarious character, with an interest in painting and the arts. But he had done the thing that so many people dream of doing and never do: he had turned his back on the civilization in which he had been trained to live, and had come north to the Barrier Reef. He had now been living on Richards Island for eleven years, most of the time entirely alone. He had grown a beard, I was told, and very rarely came to the mainland.

I asked, 'What does he do all day?'

'Well, he paints.' Nobody had any other information. There was, I noticed, a certain reserve about my friend Bassett. But I was eager to meet him. Here clearly was a man, mad or sane, who would have the answers about the beachcombing life, and I set off in a launch for Richards Island in the morning.

There had been a storm overnight, but we came up to

the lee side of the island in a subsiding sea and found an anchorage off the beach. Thick jungle came down to the water's edge, but there was a faintly defined path which led over a hill to Bassett's house on the other side of the island. Once on the path one was engulfed in that mysterious green light. Wherever there was a break in the trees tropical flowers blazed up in the sunshine, but all the rest of the way lay in shadow, and one trod on a compost of decaying leaves and the rotten trunks of fallen trees. Here and there wild scrub hens had been building incubators for their eggs—big mounds of warm mouldering leaves—and I was constantly disentangling myself from a prickly creeper that winds itself round your clothes like the tentacles of an octopus, and is called a 'wait-a-while'. There was no sound anywhere, not even the movement of a bird in the trees.

It was something of a relief then, to come out of the jungle in front of Bassett's house; and that was the first of a series of anticlimaxes I experienced that day. It was immaculate. White adobe walls, a thatched roof, bananas and poinsianas in the garden, a sandy beach on either side. No real estate agent could have dreamed of anything more spruce, more precise, more *modern* than this. And there, quietly reading in a striped canvas chair on the veranda, was Bassett himself. He looked, if anything, somewhat brisker and younger than when I had known him twenty years before. True, he had a beard, but it was nicely clipped, and instead of the traditional beachcomber's wear, the frayed duck trousers and the tattered shirt, he was wearing a smart pair of coloured shorts. Directly he heard my footsteps he got up and came forward holding out his hand.

'You won't remember me,' I began cautiously.

'But of course I do. Delighted to see you. Come and meet my wife.'

She was wearing a bright cotton dress and, like Bassett,

looked well and happy. They had been married eighteen
months before.

'I wish we could give you a drink,' she said, 'but we
haven't got any. But you must stay to lunch.'

'You don't drink?' I asked.

'Indeed we do when we can. But we have to get it from
the mainland and we haven't been over recently.'

The mainland was only a couple of hours away by launch
and I could see that they had a launch in the bay.

'When was the last time you were there?'

'I forget,' Bassett said, 'about six weeks ago I think.
It's such a business getting the launch started and then the
tide and the wind have to be right. We don't go unless
we absolutely have to.'

'What about guests? I suppose you have a lot of friends
coming over to stay?'

'Well . . . sometimes.' They sounded a little cautious
on this point, and I added: 'It's such a relief, of course,
when they go.' With that they both warmly agreed.

They had no radio (there was no electricity), no newspapers, no regular post, and although they could see Dunk
Island quite clearly on the northern horizon, they never
went there.

'I saw another house from the path on the way over
here,' I said. 'Do you see a good deal of the people
there?'

'Oh, the Joneses,' Bassett was not enthusiastic. 'No, we
don't see much of them.'

'But they are only twenty minutes away.'

'We have a slight feud with them at the moment,' his
wife explained. 'They forgot our meat last time they were
on the mainland.'

'Who *do* you meet then? Do you never go away?'

Bassett contemplated it a moment and said, 'I did go
down to Melbourne once with the idea of spending a month
or two. But it was horrible. People push you off the pave-

ment. I came back after two days. It's much pleasanter
here.'

I could see that, of course: the tropical bay was all
around us. But you cannot exist on scenery alone. For
nine years Bassett had lived here entirely by himself. His
wife had been married before, and had spent most of her
life in Melbourne and the country towns in the south. But
now that she had come to Richards Island she said she
never wanted to go back to the south again, and she could
not understand how she had endured that other life for so
long.

It was not I but the Bassetts who led the conversation
through lunch. We sat in a cool room lined with books,
eating an excellent fish salad, and they briskly touched on
such topics as the Cold War, the novels of Simenon,
cricket, the cooking of fish, Gauguin (there were one or
two prints of the Tahitian pictures on the wall), and the
carvings of the natives in New Guinea.

Bassett, on one of his rare adventures into the outside
world, had been to New Guinea, which is even wilder than
Richards Island, and he wanted to make another trip there
one day. After that we discussed Harpo Marx and the
ballet.

I returned to the attack again: 'But tell me. What do
you *do* here?'

'Do?'

'How do the days go by? Don't you get bored?'

'Yes, sometimes. But not so often as we used to in the
city. God, the incredible boredom of Melbourne and
Sydney.'

'Don't you get lonely?'

'*That* never. There's never enough time. We've just
finished building the house and there's a lot more to be
done.' He indicated his garden, a half-finished oil-painting
on an easel, the book on his lap, his boat anchored in the

bay, and beyond that the wide Pacific and the islands along the Reef.

One began to see his point; indeed, after I had been there a few more hours it was difficult to see anything but his point, and I was finding myself on the defensive. What, in fact, did I do with my time and what was so fascinating about it? The English weather? Driving in the city traffic? Cocktail parties? The radio, the movies, and the newspapers? People? Just how many of these things, Bassett wanted to know, were so enthralling after you've reached the age of forty? He was not dogmatic about it; he just wanted to know. Under his clear, quizzical eye I began to see that I must appear to him to be extremely odd, and probably rather unhappy. He pressed his advantage a little unfairly, I thought, when he pointed out that whereas he was perfectly content to stay where he was, I apparently often found it necessary to take holidays. The idea of escaping never entered his head, but it was constantly in mine. Otherwise why all this travelling?

I said: 'But where is this life *getting* you?' and regretted it at once, since clearly he might have replied by asking just where was my life getting me. But instead he said, 'Are you a Roman Catholic?'

'No.'

'Then probably you've got a Puritan conscience. You think that life here is too easy and therefore it must be wrong. You think we are getting away with something.'

'No,' I said. But the truth was I *had* expected to find him somewhat eccentric, or at least a little dissipated.

In the end we agreed rather solemnly that successful beachcombing required a certain amount of capital, at any rate to start with; and that it was impossible if one had a family of young children. And with this we took off our clothes and waded from the sand into the warm sea.

I came away that evening from Richards Island feeling

very much the odd man out, the interloper in a scene
where there was clearly a certain peace of mind. And yet
not all the answers had been given, and something somewhere was not explained.

On the way back to the mainland the man on my launch
said: 'It's lucky you got me to run you over. I'm a friend
of Bassett's.'

'Isn't everybody friendly with him?'

'They're a funny lot around here. Always bellyaching
about something.' He jerked his thumb back towards the
islands with a slight gesture of contempt.

'I suppose in some ways it's an unnatural life,' I said.

'I don't know about that,' said the boatman. 'But some
of these bastards would cut your throat if they got half a
chance.' He sounded extremely bitter.

'You take this boat,' he went on. 'She's the best boat on
the coast and I bought her. Now they're trying to cut me
out of the tourist business. Well, we'll see about that. Just
the other day . . .' It was a long rambling story, full of
fierce allusions to people I had never heard of. But the
point was clear enough: there were always feuds in the
islands. If it was not this feud, it would be another.
Island A would break off relations with Island B. Families
living on the same island would suddenly cease speaking
to one another.

'Your friend Bassett generally keeps out of it,' the
boatman said, 'but the rest of them. Jesus wept. What a
bunch.'

None of the disputes sounded very serious, and as far as
I could make out the antagonists were constantly changing
from one side to the other. But disputes apparently there
had to be. It was part of the mental climate of the coast.
And this, presumably, was the serpent in paradise. The
islands were too perfect and, for most people, the beachcombing life too warm and comfortable. A man would
settle down in some lonely bay, delighted to be away from

the herd, and content with his own company. But presently a kind of paranoia was apt to set in and all sorts of imagined grievances crept into his mind until at last he found occasion for an open quarrel. Then life became bearable once more.

I don't doubt my boatman exaggerated a good deal—he was, of course, heavily involved in the turmoil himself—and I must add, in fairness, that I personally received nothing but kindness and hospitality along the coast. But I travelled next to Hayman Island, in the Whitsunday group, and there the problem was displayed again in a tragic and much more vivid way.

I had heard a great deal about Hayman Island before I arrived there. Indeed, on the Barrier Reef it is impossible not to hear about it. A new hotel had been built there, and it was designed to promote beachcombing in a really spectacular way. Some hundreds of thousands of pounds were spent on the place, and since Queen Elizabeth and the Duke of Edinburgh were expected to pause there on their forthcoming tour of Australia it had been given permission to call itself the Royal Hayman Hotel. Nothing, apparently, had been overlooked, from the lighted swimming-pool and the cellar of imported wines to the radio telephone connecting the island to the mainland.

Indeed the place was no disappointment when one arrived. The flying-boat brought us down with a long clean splash on to the lagoon, and in a moment a launch was alongside. Its crew was dressed in striped sweaters and coloured caps that must have been inspired by Miami or the South of France.

We were taken first to a long narrow jetty which had been built out over the shelf of coral into the deep water, and on this jetty a miniature train was waiting. It was a gay little affair, such as you might see at a carnival: just two box-like carriages, painted in bright scarlet and white stripes, a petrol-driven engine, and a flat-top car in front

for the luggage. We were bundled into this toy and went
rattling down the jetty to the island. A swoop round the
corner through the overhanging jungle, a blast on the
whistle, and there we were at the hotel, surrounded by
flowering poinsianas and the Kurrawong birds. A recep-
tion staff was lined up on the miniature station to meet us.
As I was conducted by a Viennese waiter across the lawns
to my bungalow a flight of bright parrots broke through
the trees.

This bungalow, like the rest, was decorated in delicate
shades of lavender and off-biscuit, and the cupboards had
that last mark of luxury, an abundance of coat hangers.
There were but three solid walls to the building—the third
wall consisted of sliding glass doors through which one
looked out on the beach, the coral sea, and the mountains
of the surrounding islands.

No one bothered you at the hotel. You could either lurk
alone in your bungalow and your personal bit of garden
or beach, or you could make your way across the lawns to
the black glass splendours of the public rooms, where
music always seemed to be emerging in some mysterious
way out of the wall. Dinner was a function which really
required a black tie and a firm knowledge of the French
language.

By night one danced. By day you set off in one of the
launches to fish, to eat live oysters off the rocks, to explore
the neighbouring islands or look at the coral. With these
launches went picnic lunches packed in ice, and when you
fished a man was standing ready to bait your hook. The
basic tariff on Hayman Island was then around four
Australian pounds a day, and although one was besieged
with a slight feeling of unreality at times, it hardly seemed
to be an excessive price.

And yet the hotel was resented. It was resented because
it was thought to be pretentious. Australia remains pretty
nearly a classless society, and the sin of snobbery is

regarded there as more deadly than all the other seven
deadly sins put together. Any attempt to establish a privi-
leged group immediately evokes the strongest sort of
opposition; and the Royal Hayman Hotel from the very
white coats of its waiters to its glossy publicity booklets
was making just such an attempt. The owners of the place
clearly never intended to create this unhappy state of
affairs; it simply overtook them after the hotel was
built.

Several of the neighbouring islands, notably South
Molle, or Daydream Island, had accommodation for
tourists too, but they could hardly hope to compete with
Hayman's flying-boats and cocktail bars. There was no
actual quarrel between Hayman and these other islands,
just a slight feeling of wariness and tension; and most of
this feeling gathered around the question of whether or
not the guests on the other islands should be allowed to
come over from time to time and peer at the idle rich
disporting themselves around their bungalows and the
splendid swimming-pool on Hayman Island.

Mr. Ian Cutler, the young manager who was recently
appointed to take charge of the hotel, was not absolutely
against the visiting tourists. He was prepared to accept
them provided he had warning in advance. On 25 June 1952,
which was a few days before I arrived on the island, he
made a particular point of telephoning South Molle and
asking the tourists there *not* to come on that day. The
reason was that Sir John Northcott, the Governor of New
South Wales, was coming to stay on Hayman Island.
Cutler (who was once A.D.C. to the Governor) had made
a special effort to have his hotel looking at its best.

There is a curious pathos and an inevitability about the
events of the next few hours. One feels that nothing could
have averted the tragedy, and that everyone involved in
it was destined to play precisely the part he did.

The Governor and his party arrived and Cutler himself

drove them in the train down to the hotel. He then returned in the train to pick up the luggage from the end of the jetty when he observed that, on this of all days, a party of trippers had come across from South Molle island. There were about forty of them straggling down the jetty already. Cutler stopped the train and told them they could not stay: they must return to their launch. He then drove on, picked up the luggage, and started on the return journey along the jetty. Most of the trippers, after a moment's hesitation, had decided to ignore Cutler's remonstrances and were continuing on towards the shore with their backs towards the oncoming train. It was Cutler's intention to get ahead of them and remonstrate once again.

There was no railing on the jetty, and not very much room for pedestrians on either side of the tracks—something less than two feet. It was towards the middle of the jetty that the accident occurred. One of the trippers was struck by the train, a confused scramble ensued, and three people, a girl and two men, were pitched over the side into the sea, which was there very shallow and sixteen feet below the jetty. The elder of the two men, a Mr. Thomas Manders May, aged sixty, struck his head on the coral and died at once. The girl and the other man, an accountant called Stockwell, were also injured when they fell.

Cutler stopped the train and got out on to the flat top of the luggage carrier to see what was happening in the water. It was at this moment that he was struck on the head from behind and two or three men grabbed his arms and pitched him into the sea. He fell heavily beside the body of Thomas May, and fractured his ankle in several places. Now everyone began shouting and running about. Some climbed down the piers of the jetty, others came wading out from the shore. Between them they carried the dead man, the girl, and Stockwell to the beach. Cutler was left for some time lying in the water, which was much

discoloured with blood, but eventually some of his own
staff arrived and got him out.

And now suddenly, with this utterly unexpected tragedy,
the whole dream-like fabric of Hayman Island fell to
pieces. Later on, of course, things returned to normal and
the hotel with its organized routine went on its way. But
just at this moment everyone on the island was shocked
out of the ordinary courses of their lives; here was the
Douanier Rousseau tiger that had actually sprung at them
from the jungle, and the attack was all the more bewilder-
ing since they had created it themselves. Everything had
happened so quickly, and on the face of it without any good
reason whatsoever. What on earth would the Governor
think? It was an effect such as you might have with a
group of children whose games grow more and more
boisterous until, bewilderingly, the accident happens, the
window is smashed, a child is run over on the roadway;
and in a second all the gaiety has vanished into thin air.
Most of the people on the jetty that day were absurdly out
of costume for the parts they had to play. Their shorts
and coloured caps were now pathetic; the little train stood
up irrelevantly like painted cardboard on the jetty; and if
anything was needed to complete the clown-into-tears
effect it was supplied by the Kurrawong birds, which kept
circling over the scene with that mournful hoodoo cry.
Moreover, they were all isolated here on an island, and
that gave the scene an additional sense of unreality.

A young policeman called Bopf who had been sent to the
island to keep watch over Sir John Northcott now took
charge of the situation. He telephoned to his superiors on
the mainland. Next the South Molle tourists were ordered
back to their boat, the *Crest*, which put to sea and stood
off a little from the jetty, and the injured people were
carried up to the hotel. No one was allowed to leave the
island.

At 6.30 p.m. a sergeant arrived from the mainland in

the launch *Mirimar*. He had May's body placed in a lead casket and locked in a marine shed at the end of the jetty. Later that night it was taken by sea to the mainland. Meanwhile, the sergeant saw Cutler in his bed in the hotel, and then, with Constable Bopf, went on board the launch, where the South Molle passengers had been waiting all this time in a state of great uneasiness. They were interviewed one by one.

On the following day Cutler was taken by flying-boat to Brisbane, 600 miles to the south, where he entered a private hospital for a series of operations on his leg. These operations were not entirely successful; at the end he still had to use crutches. The injuries to the other two people turned out to be less serious.

The case, not unnaturally, aroused great interest along the coast, for something fundamental in the Australian attitude to life had been touched; and yet it had all been so unnecessary, so tragically trivial. There were many who may have been secretly pleased to see the Royal Hayman Island Hotel—or rather their idea of the hotel— taken down a peg. But no one I met felt really vindictive about the young manager who was so eager to put on a show for his Governor that day. His remonstrances to the intruding trippers had prodded an extremely sensitive nerve (weren't the South Molle people good enough for the Governor?); still, that tactless little outburst was understandable. He had a wife and two small children, and had done well in the Royal Australian Air Force in the war.

It was not until September 2nd, more than two months after the tragedy, that the case came up for a hearing before a police court at the little town of Prosperine, on the coast opposite the islands. Cutler, who was still on crutches, was charged with having unlawfully killed Thomas May, and he pleaded not guilty.

The case, of course, revolved around whether or not

Cutler had deliberately or negligently driven the train among the trippers so as to force them into the water; and there were many conflicting ideas about this in the evidence. The names of the people who had grabbed Cutler and flung him over after the others were never established. There was just one revealing passage, when a young New South Wales farmer called Russell Sinclair Jasprizza got up to give evidence. He was one of the tourists, and he began by saying that Cutler had made no effort to stop the train as it approached the South Molle party, and that it was moving fairly fast—eight to ten miles an hour. No alarm had been sounded. After the accident he saw Cutler get out of the driver's seat on to the flat top of the luggage carrier behind the train, where he began walking up and down. And he heard Cutler say, 'I should have knocked the whole —— lot of you over.' Then the witness said he had climbed down to assist the people in the water. He added that he heard that Cutler had been thrown into the water, but he had no knowledge of the circumstances of it. All he knew was that Cutler had made that remark: 'I should have knocked the whole —— lot of you over.'

The following dialogue then took place between Jasprizza and a Mr. Barry, Q.C., who was appearing for Cutler:

Mr. Barry: Did you see anybody enter the driving compartment of the engine and strike Cutler?

Jasprizza: No.

You are very definite about that?—Yes; I was going down the side of the jetty.

Did you see any men manhandling him?—No.

Can you tell me the name of your informant who told you that Cutler was thrown over the jetty?—No.

You don't know that either?—No.

You say you don't remember the name of your informant?—It was just conversation.

The names of those who threw Cutler into the water

were also mentioned?—No. I am sure they were not mentioned.

The passengers on the *Crest* did not separate until after midnight?—That is right.

You all went out to sea after the tragedy and came back and waited on the jetty until 11 p.m.?—Yes.

The party was on board for several hours after the tragedy?—Yes.

You knew the *Crest* was coming back to the jetty to enable police to make inquiries from passengers?—I heard that.

You knew police would be investigating May's death? —Yes.

And investigating events following his death, including the throwing in of Cutler?—Yes.

And you knew by this that some members of the party had thrown him in?—No; I only heard that some members might have thrown him in.

You realized that that might have been the subject too of police investigation?—Yes.

I suggest that, prior to the arrival of police at the *Crest*, this was discussed by the passengers.—It was mentioned.

There was some discussion?—Yes.

And was there anything like a conspiracy of silence entered into?—Not to my knowledge.

Cutler was committed for trial at the end of October, and then gave evidence for the first time. He denied that he had ever made the remark about knocking the tourists over. There was no other new witness and the jury retired at 12.15 p.m. on the second day of the trial to consider their verdict. Nothing was heard from them until 3.35 p.m., when the foreman sent out a message to the judge saying that they could not agree—and what were they to do? The judge replied that they were to stay out until they did agree. At 4.15 p.m., however, he summoned them back into court and the foreman then announced that they had still failed to agree, nor were they likely to agree if given more time. Upon this they were discharged and a new trial ordered.

At this new trial, which was held in Townsville on November 10th, the jury were out for four hours, and they returned with a verdict of not guilty. Four and a half months after the moment of catastrophe on Hayman Island, Cutler hobbled out of the court to take up his life again.

Something perhaps had been achieved, at the expense of so much anxiety and unhappiness. In one sense it was a victory for those who believed so strongly that men must remain equal, for it was announced, soon after the tragedy, that things were to be conducted in a much simpler way on Hayman Island; the tariff was cut by half. There remained others who believed in the original idea of the hotel and regretted this setback to an enterprise which was begun with so much skill and imagination. Certainly the case appeared to suggest that the moment of passion is never worth the long hard consequences, and that only by endless tact and compromise can you keep the tiger at bay. One might perhaps have established here a very useful moral, that dog does not eat dog, and that even in a beachcombing paradise men must learn to live together.

But that is not a moral that has any real support in nature, for the whole story of this enchanted coast seems to be based upon a theme of struggling opposites, of death among abundance. In the teeming marine life along the Great Barrier Reef there is just one law, and that is the law of the survival of the fittest. And with all its injustice and inequality the struggle seems likely to go rolling on till Doomsday. Beachcombing is something quite apart; it is an art which requires but does not necessarily create a contented mind.

CHAPTER NINE

Bear into Albatross

DURING my schooldays in Australia my family moved house at least a dozen times. It was a mania with them, the revival of some dark nomadic instinct, and in the case of my mother it extended to the interiors of the houses as well. She adored moving furniture. When my father had gone off to work in the morning she would be seized with some new whim; housework, shopping, and all else were abandoned while she converted the dining-room into a 'sun-room' or moved the second bedroom into the attic. If father chanced to come home late at night and undressed in the dark so that he should not wake my mother, the chances were that he would find himself stepping into the wardrobe instead of the bed, or fouling a new stool which she had artlessly placed in the middle of the room. Then we were all wakened by father's cry of pain and rage. But it never made any difference to mother. Once, when we had just moved into another place in Melbourne, we found her mounted on a step-ladder in the hall, palette and brushes in hand. She had taken a dislike to the floral pattern of the wallpaper and was altering the petals of each flower to a warm shade of pink known as 'vieux rose'. It took her two days but she finished it.

These various moves of ours were always in the city—either in Sydney or Melbourne—and the odd thing is that while I can remember each of our homes quite well, the rest of my life, what I did at school, the comings and goings with the neighbours' children, and all the other aspects of my life in the city, remain a blur, disordered in time and place. Like any other child I identify each particular place by the incidents that happened there. There was the day the dead branch of a tree fell on father; the time I tumbled into the shark-infested waters of Sydney Harbour; the collision in the car, and so on. But the generality of our days, all the movements and meaning of the city, has made no lasting impression on my memory. Just occasionally an advertisement from a hoarding on a railway station, or perhaps a motor-car (the De Dion Bouton 1917 model), will be evoked by some obscure chain of coincidence, but all the rest is lost.

With the Australian bush it is absolutely different. I have only to fix my mind on some holiday by the sea, or some excursion into the Grampian Mountains, and every detail leaps to my mind with the clarity of the scene I see before me now, as I am writing, a tangle of back gardens near Regent's Park in London. In an instant I can make all these chimney-pots and scraggy walls dissolve into a wide Australian plain with the noise of sheep-dogs barking, the dust rising from the horses' hooves and the medicinal scent of eucalyptus in the air. There was a quality of excitement and revealed truth in the bush which we never experienced in the city; and this was not only because we were city children, but because the bush itself was still so untouched and so little known. To some extent everyone who went there was an explorer. You could not walk for half a mile without coming upon things which were unknown in Europe or anywhere else, and they were not recorded in any of the books we were given at school. Tennyson and Spenser were a million miles away from the bandicoot and the forests of golden wattle trees that ran up every valley. A few of the local poets had sung about the waratah, the blood-red lily which is shaped like an artichoke, the gullies filled with tree-ferns, the bell-birds, and the immemorial gum-trees, but most of it was not very good poetry.

The Australian painters were much better in their way; in the Melbourne gallery there were many bush scenes by Arthur Streeton, Hans Heyson, Penleigh Boyd, and Harold Herbert, but the majority of the local artists were still imitative and limited to illustration; they evoked very little beyond the scene itself. My mother, for example, a diligent amateur for many years, only occasionally painted from life. She was encouraged by her master to do copies, and her *chef d'œuvre* was painted from a well-known genre piece 'Across the Black Soil Plains'. It revealed a team of horses dragging a wagon-load of wool bales across the empty landscape in the sheep country to the north. This canvas, a large oblong affair in a heavy gilt frame, followed us through all our moves from house to house, and usually found a place above the sitting-room mantelpiece. We used to criticize it very unkindly, but I expect it did something to fix our ideas on 'the out-back'.

We read Australian short stories by Henry Lawson and others, but I cannot remember being told any folk-lore about the bush (though it was beginning in the hundreds of yarns and tall stories that passed from mouth to mouth), and although a good deal of scientific research was going on very little of it reached us children. So there was not much to help us, either by the way of philosophy, science, or art, to understand the oddities we saw; one simply went out into the bush and observed for oneself.

Here it was in its infinite oldness. The earth we trod on was dry land, and already old when most of Europe and Asia was submerged beneath the sea. But no one had been here before, if you excepted the blackfellows; and we certainly did except them. Through geological ages all this extraordinary fauna and flora had been living and dying here unnoticed; and it was unmarked by any kind of civilization. No wonder we loved the bush. One stepped forth as an adventurer.

One of my very earliest memories is of those intermin-

"Across the Black Soil Plains." My mother's copy of an oil painting showing a wagon-load of wool bales being dragged across the empty plains in the interior

able train journeys which brought us back to the city after we had been visiting Uncle Bill. The luggage racks above our heads were filled with the bags of apples, the 'specimens' (of beetles, or rocks, or flowers), and the bunches of aromatic gum leaves we had gathered through the day. The train jogged on through the darkness, stopping and starting, the vapour of our breaths congealed on the window panes, and I leaned against my mother's knee, thirsty, exhausted, and very dirty. But this mattered nothing; I had been ranging the hills all day, breaking new ground, and I had actually seen a kookaburra diving on a snake. And now I was sailing back to port with the booty: the dead lizard in the cardboard box, the jam-jar full of frog-spawn that would hatch into tadpoles by and by, and the chunk of rock with the yellow specks that might easily turn out to be gold.

As time went on and we ventured further on long walking trips through the hills, we grew familiar with things that would have seemed as strange as anthropothagi to a foreign eye. The kookaburra, the bird that shouts with gusts of hoarse, guttural laughter, was always there; but we also knew the rare black swans and white eagles. There was the lyre bird, who danced for his mate on a mound of leaves, and who was gifted with such a power of mimicry that he could exactly reproduce the sound of an axe chopping into wood, and anything else that took his fancy. There was another bird which made a noise like the crack of a stockman's whip, and there were wild cherry trees on which the pips grew, conveniently, *outside* the fruit.

We had no monkeys or savage animals, but we had the platypus, a weird, sleek, furry creature which came straight from the beginning of the world. It had fur and a broad bill like a duck, and it lived in the waterholes of the creeks. It laid eggs, and when they hatched, suckled its young. Then there were the opossums, the ant-eaters, the goannas, and a certain spiked lizard called the *Moloch horridus*, which changed the colour of its warty skin, wholly or in patches, from yellow to grey or red.

We had only to go to a place called Phillip Island, an hour or two away from Melbourne, and there in a game reserve we could roam all day among birds and animals which others might only dream of all their lives. Phillip Island was and still is a fantasy of Australian wild life; one goes there to see the seals, the penguins, the mutton birds, and the koala bears that perch in trees.

Each species has its definite place on the island. The seals come into Seal Rocks, off the south-eastern tip of the shore, and they breed in thousands. On a calm day you can take a boat and sail among them. On any day you can stand on the cliffs and watch them basking, roaring, fighting, mating, waddling, and diving from the rocks; and that particularly pungent smell, a leathery, salty smell with strong undertones of decayed fish, travels powerfully across the sea. The seals never achieve the superb frolicsome grace of the dolphins in the water, but they make a wonderful sight here in the open ocean, and sometimes you will see them gliding about in dozens just a few inches below the surface. In the mating season the uproar on the rocks is continuous. There is not really enough room for them all, but the fierce old males clear a space for their young wives and then stand guard, swaying from side to side and bellowing ferociously whenever any bachelor comes near. They fight, like all-in wrestlers, with fearful gruntings and groanings and in deadly seriousness. The next generation depends upon the outcome, for the young females will certainly go off with any new champion who can defeat their husband. However, if he wins they stay; and often you will see the old man emerge from the fray with glorious scars on his flanks. He stands for a moment on the edge of the rock, still bellowing defiance, and then, like Thomas Grey's Welsh bard hurling curses on the

English hosts, he launches himself into the abyss and hits the sea with a mighty splash, his flippers pinned along his sides.

For a time there was a wild slaughter of these seals—something like a quarter of a million of them were killed for their oil and skins in the Phillip Island area in the early years of last century—but now they are protected. The sea-elephant, like the mammoth kangaroo whose remains are preserved in fossils, is now extinct in Australian waters, but the Antarctic gales blow in here directly from the South Pole, and sometimes they bring with them the white seal, a beautiful creature who looks very much as Rudyard Kipling described him in the *Jungle Book*. He rarely comes ashore.

The rookeries of the mutton birds—the *Puffinus pacificus* —lie close by on the island. The mutton bird, or, if you like, the wedgetailed shearwater, will never know the glories of the albatross's flight—that effortless tilting of the ten-foot wings that will carry an albatross straight into the blast of a fifty mile an hour wind—but he has at least a miraculous sense of timing, and his moral attitudes are impeccable. He is like a small duck, dark chocolate in colour, except for his reddish hooked bill, and he ranges the Pacific Ocean in communities of millions. Precisely at dusk in mid-September each year the mutton birds return to Phillip Island. Just a few of them arrive: these are the pilot birds, and immediately on alighting they set about clearing out the nesting burrows on the cliffs. Then they vanish again into the open sea until the third week in November.

It is usually in a gale (known as the 'mutton bird gale') and usually about November 25th that the main swarm suddenly appears like a rain cloud across the sea and settles on the island. There is much confusion. Every couple wants the same burrow that it had last year, every bachelor wants a new burrow and a mate. Even when they sort themselves out (which they never entirely succeed in doing), there is a great deal of work to be done in clear-out the burrows and establishing themselves. The shuf-flings, the quarrellings, and the matings go on all night on this and every other night. Only the days are peaceful, for the whole community takes off before dawn and through the daylight hours ranges the sea in search of squid and small fish. Directly they return in the evening the uproar breaks out afresh.

The act of mating is rather pathetic. It is the male which makes the advances. He approaches the female with wings half-spread and he utters a low, yearning cry. It is then up to the female to take her decision: if she likes him she stands her ground, and presently the two birds nestle affectionately together with little cooing noises: if not, she simply turns her back and walks away, leaving the male mewing there, a little absurdly, with his wings still lifted and, no doubt, with rage and mortification in his heart.

The eggs arrive through the summer—one egg to each couple—and the parents take turn and turn about in minding it, one bird fishing while the other sits on the egg. When the young one hatches out, a feeble bundle of soft down, they take turns in feeding it. The fidelity of the mutton birds is, indeed, remarkable; by placing identifica-tion rings on their legs it has been established that they will always return to the same burrow every year, and a marriage is a marriage for life.

In mid-April the parents take off in a body, leaving the young birds behind them. But by now the young have grown feathers and are able to face life on their own. They approach the proposition very unwillingly. For a few days they hang about the burrows living on their fat, and then they begin to make a few trial runs down the sandy ramps that serve as launching platforms. Finally they take off into the sky. It must be an exhilarating moment when the hungry young bird, without any other instruction than his own instinct, dives and snaps up his first fish from the sea. Within ten days of the parents' departure the young are all on the wing, and then they too vanish, no one knows where, on the wide winds of the Pacific until the following September.

Mutton birds are still killed and salted away in casks. But the flesh is oily and not very good to eat, and now on Phillip Island they are protected by law.

Perhaps the mutton birds might be better known than they are were it not for the more elegant penguins. The penguins, the small fairy penguin of the Pacific, also come to Phillip Island in great numbers, and their chosen spot is a wide sandy beach a little further round to the east. The best moment to see them is just before dusk in the summer. You sit down very quietly in the sand dunes, much as you would take a seat in the stalls of the theatre, and indeed the scene which is about to unfold before you can be as enchanting and as moving as a ballet. For a time, while your senses grow more acute, nothing unusual happens, just the tumble and slither of the long Pacific rollers and the light breeze along the empty beach. Then you notice the seagulls, the villains of the piece, gathering on the wet tidal sand on the right; and about the same time you hear an indistinct barking coming from the sea. Then, on the edge of the beach, just at the point where the waves are making a tangle of white lace on the sand, ten or perhaps a dozen little ninepins pop into view. They stand in a row, barking, white chests thrust out, flippers akimbo, and facing the shore. Presently another group, and another and another, appear out of the sea, and they stand there nervously and indecisively, listening and waiting. At last one bolder than the rest waddles slowly forward and the others reluctantly follow.

This is the signal for the gulls. They know, from a thousand other evenings, that the penguins' crops are full of fish which they are bringing home for their young in the burrows among the sand dunes. They know the penguin is a nervous bird, and that when frightened he will disgorge his fish and bolt back into the sea. So now they wheel up into the air and come down in relays, like diving bombers, on to the penguins on the sand. You see all this in the last light of evening, when there is only a silver glow in the sky so that everything is rather indistinct. One thing only is apparent: the beach is suddenly empty again. It is impossible to know how many fish the wicked gulls have taken, and how many penguins got back into the sea with the day's catch; but by now your sympathies are engaged entirely, you want to drive off the gulls and encourage the penguins to come on again out of the sea. In each burrow in the dunes behind you two blind penguin chicks, covered with down, are waiting, and the chances are that they will die if their parents do not get home.

The gulls make one last circuit over the beach before darkness settles down, and then depart. This is the moment to shine a torch towards the waves—for some reason the penguins do not fear it—and it is an enormous pleasure to see them pop up again, first a dozen, then thirty or forty, until finally a whole army of them is standing there in long lines on the wet sand. They pause for another minute or two, and then, with **many** hesitations, come waddling up the beach **directly towards** you. Wherever you shine the torch you see large groups on the move, all marching very closely together, and moving with excruciating difficulty. No woman hurrying home exhausted with her shopping basket through the evening crowds is so pathetic as these frightened and ridiculous little birds. Their crops are so distended that they tumble over in every unexpected footprint in the sand. For a moment they lie there helpless, and then painfully struggle back on to their feet and battle on again. As they come **on**

Information Service Australia House, London

"They stand in a row, barking, white chests thrust out, flippers akimbo, facing the shore." Penguins coming up the beach in the torchlight on Phillip Island

towards you up the beam of torchlight they keep thrust-
ing out their beaks in little jerks, as though they were
listening for some new danger in the darkness.

Now you yourself, sitting there watching, are the
menace. If you cough or move they will stand stock-still
in an instant. Another sound and they will bolt, possibly
disgorging their fish as they go. And on the night I
watched this happened. For some minutes one of the
women in the party had been struggling with a cough that
was rising in her throat. Heaven knows she intended no
harm, and tried to fight it back; but when the leading birds
were barely twenty feet away it overmastered her. At once
the birds stopped. Then, while she pressed her handkerchief to her mouth and coughed again, they turned sideways. At the third cough they bolted. They ran towards
the sea in a disordered rout beyond the range of the
torchlight, and we could not see what damage had been
done.

It was a full ten minutes before they came up the beach
again, and now they appeared to be quite desperate. One
group headed directly for the torch, with a particularly big
bird in front. He came right up to us and stood, not six
inches from my foot. He must have known we were there,
for he stood for a long time peering at us uncertainly.
And then, reassured, he went on between us into the darkness of the sand dunes, and the others followed on behind.
They came plodding through like a procession of mourners
at a funeral, in utter silence, and they were so near that at
any moment one had only to reach forward to touch them.
Close at hand they looked, if anything, more absurd and
pathetic than before; they were so tired, so nearly home,
so overwhelmingly anxious to get there. All the sand in
the circle of torchlight was criss-crossed with the webbed
footprints of their feet.

When an hour had gone by and the last of them was
home from the sea we got stiffly to our feet. We could hear

all around us in the burrows the squawkings and exclamations of the young fledglings gobbling down the fish as it came from their mothers' crops, and demanding more. As we came up the cliff face I nearly tripped over one straggler who had apparently made his burrow rather further away than the others. He made no attempt to run—he was too close to home. He hissed at me angrily and went plodding on his way.

There remain the koala bears to see on Phillip Island, not very many of them, but you would be unlucky if you did not find at least half a dozen on a morning's walk through the gum trees at any time of the year. There they perch, about the size of a two-year-old human baby, and you would have to be a monster not to be moved by that rubber nose, the tufted ears, the two black-button eyes, the thick grey pelt, and that air of infinite benignity. The tree bear is the most inoffensive of all creatures, and it is quite defenceless. It asks of life simply a convenient fork in a gum tree where it can repose its woolly behind all day while it sleeps, and at night a supply of fresh gum leaves. Without ambition or hate or envy or affectation of any kind it likes to sit there quietly meditating, and it is precisely what it is—a teddy bear. If you pick up one that is accustomed to human beings it will reach up its arms to you like a baby and nestle on your lap, with its claws holding on to your shoulder. If you frighten it or hurt it in any way it will cry piteously.

By night the koala climbs to the topmost branches for the most succulent leaves, and when they are finished he will descend gravely to the ground and amble across to the next tree. He climbs the trunk by putting his arms and legs around it and proceeding upward in a series of little jumps like a linesman mounting a telegraph pole. His single child is born in June, and spends the first three months either in its mother's pouch or on her back with his claws holding on tightly to the thick wool in the same

Information Service Australia House, Lon

"Without ambition or hate or envy or affectation of any kind
it likes to sit there quietly meditating, and it is precisely what
it is—a teddy bear"

"Her single child is born in June"

way as a child will hold on when being given a piggy-back. After three months he is too heavy to carry and the mother dumps him off on a fork of the branches to fend for himself.

There were days on Phillip Island when the bears used to come round in quite large numbers. We had a camp close to the sea, and sometimes when we looked out in the morning they would be curled up in all the trees around the tent. They showed no fear. When we called to them they looked down sleepily for a moment and then relaxed again comfortably. I spent most of one day when I was ill in bed observing a bear. Absolutely nothing happened. Then in the evening he stretched himself with a sigh, and without moving his position, reached up a claw for a handful of gum leaves and began munching. I never saw the bears drink anything, and when I come to think of it I never saw them *do* anything in the slightest degree unusual. I do not know a single story about a koala bear. There is an imperishable lassitude in that innocence. It is the nearest thing on this earth to a state of Buddhist nirvana.

As you would expect, the life-force in the bear is not very strong. Confronted by any sudden disaster he utters that pathetic high-pitched cry and then, improvidently, dies. The bush-fires catch him and burn him up. He is apt to contract a nasty chill in the winter and collapse with pneumonia. He is susceptible to ophthalmia, periostitis of the skull (that empty skull), and a number of other diseases. If his supply of chosen gum leaves runs out (and he will only eat certain kinds), he simply gives up and dies. With such disasters all around him there has been a grave danger at times that the race would become extinct. In recent years, however, game wardens have been able to do a good deal in securing their supply of food and keeping the worst menaces, such as fires and human beings, at bay. One hopes very much that they will succeed in cherishing the bear, for there are no other species like him. He may be indolent and even a slight bore, but he remains certainly the most endearing creature on earth.

It seems hard to believe that there could exist in the same country, let alone on the same island, anything so loathsome as the snake. I do not know whether Australian snakes are more vicious than in any other country, but there are over a hundred different varieties, many of them deadly poisonous. The Australian snake is everything the bear is not, and he multiplies in millions. The fear of snakes was inbred in us, and it was an instinctive act to kill them wherever we could. Even as young children we learned how to give first-aid treatment for a snake bite: you first tied a tourniquet on the patient's arm or leg to delay the flow of poison to the heart. Then you took a penknife or a razor blade and made an incision between the two punctures from the snake's fangs, and provided all your teeth were sound you sucked the poisoned blood out of the wound. Finally you rubbed some Condy's crystals into the wound and took the patient off to a doctor. It was important not to twist the tourniquet too tightly lest you stopped the flow of blood entirely (which might mean that the patient lost his arm), and that the patient should not run about (which would hasten the flow of poison to his heart). We knew these things very well, but the knowledge did nothing much to allay the peculiar dread we felt, that sudden spasm of the heart, when we saw coiled on the ground at our feet a brown or a tiger snake poising his head to strike. Made clumsy by fear one would beat at him again and again with a stick until long after he was dead.

I had a friend called Boddington, or some such name, and with him this fear of snakes had developed into an obsession. Indeed he had good reason; as a child he had been bitten by a tiger snake and so long a time elapsed before he was given treatment that his heart was affected. For years afterward his head would suddenly begin to spin, and unless he was given brandy or a stimulant of some kind he would faint. This was a fearful embarrassment to him, because he was an exceptionally good athlete, and his doctor gave orders that before entering into any contest he should have a tot of brandy. Like so many other boys he had a horror of being 'different', and before a football match began he would skulk about the locker room until no one was looking and then swallow his draught. In later years this physical disability wore off, but the mental effect of the bite remained. It took the curious form of giving him a mania about snakes, a kind of love-hate. He collected snakes. He had specimens preserved in bottles all round his study, and long lines of skins tacked to the wall. He had gathered a formidable library upon the subject, and read every new snake book that came out. He was, in fact, a bore about snakes and talked of them whenever he could.

Boddington related all this to me one night when we were on a camping holiday on Phillip Island. I asked him what he thought the effect would be if he were ever bitten again. 'I couldn't stand it,' he said simply. 'I know what would happen because I have thought of it often. I would die with shock on the spot.'

He was bitten the next day. He had gone down to the waterhole where we shaved and had perched his mirror on top of a post. With an accidental movement he knocked the mirror into the long grass, and then, when he reached down his hand to retrieve it he saw the two furious yellow eyes, the forked tongue darting out, the open jaws with two pointed fangs and the long slender neck poised ready to strike. Boddington might still have had time to move his arm but he was quite paralysed. He could not even bring himself to cry out. Then the snake lashed forward and bit him on the forearm, not far from the spot where he had been bitten as a small boy.

It was probably the pain that brought him out of his

trance. The snake had vanished into the grass, and he turned and walked quite slowly up to the house. By the time we others reached him he was an awful sight. He had turned pale green under the shaving soap on his cheeks, and all he could do was point to the two little drops of blood oozing from his arm. I do not suppose we handled him very well. We all knew the treatment required, but there is such a difference between theory and practice, and with a snake bite one is always agitated by the thought that unless you act quickly and correctly your patient will be dead in half an hour. We tied a handkerchief around his arm, but the question was—how tight should it be? We tied it a little tighter to make sure. Then again, with the razor, how deep did you cut? We decided to cut a little deeper. The rest of the business we managed well enough (except none of us knew how long you should go on sucking the wound), and someone went off for the doctor. While we waited Boddington said nothing at all. Just once he made a sign that he wanted water. His hand was shaking so badly that I had to hold the glass to his lips, and even then his teeth rattled loudly on the rim. When finally the doctor arrived and took him away in a car I must confess I never expected to see Boddington again.

Yet he was back an hour later, miraculously restored. He ate a hearty lunch and from that moment proceeded with his holiday in the best of spirits. When I met him long afterwards and asked him how his famous collection of snakes and snake books was getting on he answered laconically, 'I've sold it,' and he changed the subject. It seemed too simple a psychological story to be true, but as far as I know Boddington was never again a bore about snakes. He took up golf, and was killed, I heard, by a Japanese bullet in New Guinea in the last war.

After the snakes I think the things we most dreaded were the bush fires. Perhaps dreaded is not the right word, because there was such an operatic grandeur about them,

such a quality of awful catastrophic doom, that one was
excited and frightened, cowardly and heroic, all at the
same time. It was not at all like the bombing in the war
because then one felt that in the last resort it could be
stopped; the bombs were released by a human agency that
was susceptible to reason and control. But a bush fire was
beyond all reason. It was blind malignant fate, and it was
bound to run its senseless, useless course to the bitter end.

Sometimes the bush fires were terrible; a whole mountain-side would blaze up in a hot north wind, and the speed
and direction of the flames were the same as the wind
itself. It is true that most of the fires were started through
carelessness—a lighted match flung down among the gum
leaves, a spark from a locomotive, an unextinguished camp
fire, even a broken bottle acting as a magnifying glass on
the sun's rays—but once begun the fire had a life of its
own. It advanced in a growling, terrifying wall and it was
quite pitiless. The church bell would ring, the farmers
would rush out with wet sacks and green branches to beat
out the flames, but if it was a bad fire and their wooden
homes lay in its path there was nothing much they could
do except pray for a sudden miraculous change of wind.
It's a despairing business, fighting a fire; smoke fills your
eyes and lungs, the heat is unbearable, and there comes a
moment when one is overtaken by a feeling of hopeless-
ness: this monster is too big. You drive it back in one place
only to discover that it has leapt up behind you, and there
and there, and over there. One feels an immense desire to
give way to inertia, to let the fire rage on and do its
worst.

In a high wind of thirty or forty miles an hour there is
no chance of running away. You first hear the noise from
a long way off, smoke begins to blot out the sun, and then
suddenly the fire is on you. Sometimes you will see sparks
and great balls of flame, rushing through the sky fifty feet
or more above the ground, and well ahead of the main

body of the fire. Looking up you see nothing but the sky afire above your head and showers of sparks cascading down. These balls of flame appear to bounce from one tree-top to another until all the top of the forest is ablaze; and then the ground fire comes on and demolishes the saplings and the undergrowth below. It makes an indescribable roar, something like an oncoming tidal wave perhaps, but punctuated every now and then by a specially loud explosion, when a really big eucalyptus tree comes down. Often these trees will go up like a torch as though they had exploded by internal combustion. First the foliage takes fire, then the whole trunk glows red until it crashes headlong to the ground.

As you would expect, cattle and sheep go mad. They turn first in one direction, then another with frightened staring eyes, until they lose their wits entirely and stampede directly into the flames or simply sink to their knees waiting to be burnt alive. As for the wild animals, all their fear of human beings is forgotten in the overmastering fear of the fire. You see them come bounding out of the bush as their lairs burn up behind them, wallabies, wild dogs, and other creatures which you have never glimpsed before, and they run into the farmyards believing pathetically that they can find protection there. Even the snakes have no thought of attacking, and it is not unknown for them to join a farmer and his family in a waterhole— the water lukewarm and full of sparks—until the worst of the fire is over.

Then afterwards, if the family survives, as somehow it usually does, the farmer is confronted with an appalling sight: the house burnt down to its one brick chimney, the iron water-tanks twisted like paper, the water itself evaporated in steam, and all the stockyards covered with thick black ash. For a long time the ground is so hot that one feels the heat coming up through the soles of a thick country boot. It does not matter how green the crop or the vegetable gardens, everything burns, even down to the very metal of the cooking-pots.

These fires can go on for days or even weeks, and by night they make a beautiful sight. If you chance to watch from a long way off you will see a great patch of yellow and red creeping steadily along the mountain-side. It eats its way forward in fits and starts, dying down for a moment and then flaring up again, and a bright sunset glow is reflected in the sky. Even in the cattle country of the interior and the far north where there are so few trees, there are fires among the grass. A plant called tumble-weed, which detaches itself from the ground and blows along in the wind to scatter its seed, will pile up against the fences. Then some accident happens, some simple thing like a rat igniting the phosphorus tip of a wax match with its sharp teeth, and up goes the ominous spiral of smoke across the plain.

January and February, the midsummer months, were the season for bush fires, and then in the winter, especially in June and July, we got the floods. There is nothing quite so dismal as the aftermath of a flood—the filth and stench of the mud lying two or three inches deep over the carpets and furniture of a house—but on the whole the floods were not so bad as the fires. I can even remember enjoying them very much. For a boy it was a splendid thing to go boating down the main street of the town, to see uprooted trees cannonading against the piles of a rickety bridge, and best of all to watch a house gradually loosen from its foundations in the current. It waddles like a duck for a moment and then sedately enters the stream, slowly gyrating on its own axis, with chickens and perhaps the owners perching on the roof; and they are borne away miserably shouting and gesticulating into the open ocean of the plains.

The locust and the grasshopper plagues were another fine spectacle, provided of course that it was not *your* land they were invading. They arrived in unbelievable teeming billions, so many of them that they made a stain in the unclouded sky like the smoke of a bush fire and the noise of their wings was like an oncoming express train. The settlers used to light oil fires and rush into the open shouting and banging upon kerosene tins, but if the locusts were really determined nothing would stop them. They billowed down on the ground in such numbers that it was impossible to walk about without crushing them horribly beneath your feet, and the foliage of the trees shivered under the movement of millions of working jaws. It was an insanity of hunger. Within an hour or two the swarm would rise again and there would be nothing left but the bare earth (where perhaps a two-foot crop had been standing before) and the skeletons of the trees. Even the very bark of the branches would be eaten.

I do not wish to suggest that we were for ever surrounded by these disasters, or that they were worse or more frequent than anywhere else. Over the seven-tenths of the continent which was quite uninhabited the elements raged as they had always done without harming anybody. It was only in the regions where we were trying to upset the arrangements of Nature by introducing European plants and domestic animals that the damage was done. Nature fought back relentlessly. When the indigenous trees were cut down to make room for grass she set up a dust bowl. When the settlers were deluded by a run of good seasons into over-stocking their properties, a drought would come along and wipe them out. If the desert was irrigated for the growing of vines and citrus fruits, the young plants would thrive splendidly for a time; and then some deficiency of salts would develop in the soil or the locusts would arrive. And quite apart from such pests as the cattle tick that somehow crossed the ocean from abroad, there were Australian diseases with their own peculiar virulence.

The sheep stations were probably the first to emerge successfully from this struggle. For some reason the Merino sheep flourishes in Australia as it does nowhere else on earth, and its wool is the finest that there is. When I first used to go up to the sheep country some twenty-five years ago, many of the station owners were already rich, and the price of wool has risen to astronomical heights since then.

The station I used to visit was not very big, about fifty thousand acres. It lay in the vast inland plain known as the Riverina between the Murrumbidgee and the Murray rivers in New South Wales, and it was called Cocket-geedong. I am not absolutely certain about the spelling of this name, but at any rate it meant Cocky Sit Down, which was the phrase the natives used to explain that flocks of cockatoos would often light down here to feed on the salt pans, especially during the wet season. There was a stone homestead standing among a grove of parched she-oaks, and the landscape consisted simply of bare monotonous plains that stretched away to the horizon. There were very few roads or fences: the sheep roamed about more or less at will for months on end until they were rounded up, to be shorn, branded, and castrated, and then sent out into the wilderness again.

In that isolation one soon got to know the people on a station as one grows to know the passengers and the crew of a ship. There was the owner or the manager and his family, who lived at the homestead with the book-keeper, the stable-boys, and the jackaroos. There were the boundary-riders who rode about the extremities of the station in wide-brimmed hats, a whip over their shoulders, and their 'tucker'—hunks of bread and cold mutton—tucked into the saddle bags. Always at least one sheep-dog ran at their heels, and often you would see them, man, horse, and dog, jogging away in a slow ambling canter to some fixed point in the infinite distance.

I loved watching the sheep-dogs. They responded only

to their masters, and the language was a low penetrating whistle hissed between the man's teeth. At one sound the dog would lie flat and motionless on the ground, at another he would gallop away to head off the mob in a new direction. An old dog seldom needed any instructions at all; he would trot along all day in a swinging motion behind the sheep, always keeping them moving at a settled pace, until at last in the evening he piloted them through a gateway and left them there for the night. The dogs never bit the sheep—they were usually shot if they did— nor as a rule did they bark; they simply ran up to the stragglers in a threatening way and that was all that was necessary. Just occasionally when a big, close-packed mob was on the move one would see a delightful thing: to save himself a long run round the outskirts the dog would head directly across the mob, bounding with complete assurance from one woolly back to another until he reached the other side. It was the dogs who really managed the mustering, and no station could have got along without them.

Then once a year the shearers arrived, and in those days they were some of the roughest and the toughest characters in the whole Australian scene. They used to follow the shearing season southward. It was even said that some of them began in Queensland in the far north, where the summer started early, and then moved down from one station to another, shearing as they went, until they reached the southern coasts of Victoria. Then they took ship for New Zealand and sheared their way down through the North Island to the South as far as Dunedin; and there they went to bed for the three winter months with a girl and a couple of cases of whisky. Then rising like giants refreshed at the first breath of spring, penniless but determined, they took passage as stewards and deckhands in the freighters plying to Queensland, and the annual cycle began again.

They made large sums of money. In those days when a

pound had twice or three times the buying power it has
now, they earned thirty-two shillings and sixpence a
hundred sheep, and a good man would shear more than
that in a day, even with hand-shears which were still in
use.[1]

Inflation has scarcely impeded the shearer. Nowadays a
shearer's cook can expect to get up to £80 a week, which
is more no doubt than the shearers themselves receive;
but then cooks are something of a rarity in Australia, like
prima donnas or talented jockeys. A cook on a coastal
freighter is often paid more than the captain.

While he is working—and the shearer lives a hard and
uncomfortable life—there is little on which he can spend
his money except food. It is between jobs, when his pocket
is full of notes and he heads for the nearest town, that he
likes to spend his money; and then begins the lost weekend. Australian country pubs were much drearier then
than they are now: long dark saloons with the counters
awash with beer and ageing flyblown advertisements on
the wall. But they constituted all heaven for the shearer
coming in from the arid bush, and they were equipped to
deal with men who wished to drink themselves through
the various stages of hilarity and bellicosity until they
reached stupor and forgetfulness at last. I remember at
Cocketgeedong they spoke with awe of the Saturday night
when the wool sheds of three neighbouring stations happened to 'cut-out' (to finish shearing) at the same moment,
and over a hundred shearers converged upon the town of
Jerilderie together. There was then only one policeman at
Jerilderie and half a dozen pubs. It was only when the beer
ran out that the party ended.

But it was the actual shearing of the sheep which seemed
to my nurtured city eye so appalling. The animals were so

[1] The new world record was established in New Zealand in January
1953 by a Mr. Godfrey Bowen, a saw-miller who shears sheep as a
hobby. He sheared 456 animals in nine hours.

stupid, so incredibly helpless. For months they roamed in arcady of a kind, unmolested by anyone. Now suddenly they were driven together in a terrifying confusion of dust and noise. They cried out panic-stricken but it was no use; one after another they were grabbed with rough hands, flung on their backs, and the thick silky pelts were shaved off them as though they were so many bananas being skinned. The wool rarely came away clean; nearly every sheep was nicked and even deeply cut by the shears. Then a tarred stick would be jabbed into the wounds and the running blood, and the animal was driven naked into the yards. If it chanced to be cold that night there was always a percentage that died.

The castration was even worse. Only a small number of rams was required; all the rest were submitted to a crude operation with the knife. But the shock was always too much for some of the sheep, and the baa-ing of those that survived could be heard from a long way off as you rode across the plain. Compared to this operation the red-hot branding and the 'dipping' of the sheep in a chemical bath seemed to be relatively humane.

None of this, of course, applied to the prize ram. Then as now he was extremely valuable. He was the lord of all, and the comforts of an Oriental pasha were lavished on him. His virility was immense; it was even said (I do not know with how much truth) that a ram could serve some forty sheep in a night. We knew nothing of artificial insemination then (with all the paraphernalia of aeroplanes which now fly the test-tubes and the scientists to the distant stations), but already it was no uncommon thing for several thousand pounds to be paid for a champion ram, and already there was being forced upon the Australian sheep a civilization as confined, as ruthless, and often as sterile as the life of the bee or the white ant.

Each year in the stock-yards the sheep were sorted out; those that were to die, those few which were to be allowed to keep up the life stream of the herd, and the great majority which were condemned to a sterile routine of producing wool and food; and none were free. There are so many sheep in Australia (over a hundred million at the last counting) that death has to overtake them very rapidly, as it does occasionally in a drought, for the loss of a few hundred thousand to be noticed. The system is entirely designed so that only the fittest shall survive. In Australia one always thinks of sheep in the plural, as a vast nameless mass, and I remember how astonished and derisive I was when I came to England and the Mediterranean and saw shepherds actually *minding* sheep, miserable threadbare flocks; and some of the animals—this was the really astounding thing—were known by individual names. Perhaps then I began to understand for the first time some of the Biblical parables of the Lamb. Up to that point sheep were, for me, simply sheep, as ants are ants, and certainly beyond the range of human compassion.

I inquired about Cocketgeedong and the other Riverina stations when I went back to Australia on a trip in 1952; and it seems that things have altered a good deal. They no longer see, as we used to do occasionally, great droves of kangaroos bounding away into the scrub, perhaps fifty or more of them at a time. The sheep-dogs persist but the boundary riders tend to move about by car or motor-cycle. And the team of Clydesdales that used to cart the wool from the shearing shed to the railway a dozen miles away —that has vanished entirely. I regret these horses very much. They were one of the immemorial scenes of the Australian bush, and I can never now go to a country show or see a brewer's wagon in a city street without remembering them.

They had a team of a dozen at Cocketgeedong, all mares, with superb chestnut rumps and massive necks that rose like the arches of a bridge. When the wool came from the shed it was pressed into big oblong hessian sacks, each one about the size of the smaller stones in the Egyptian pyramids, and these were loaded on to a flat-topped wooden wagon. When the pile had risen some twenty feet high, and indeed resembled a small pyramid, the horses were whipped up and the whole cavalcade went bowling across the empty plains to the railway. It was a scene, in fact, which was very much as mother had painted it in her copy of 'Across the Black Soil Plains'.

There is nothing in the world quite so benign and fore-bearing as the Clydesdales—nothing that quite gives that impression of mild, shapely strength; and I might always have thought of them in that way if I had not been at Cocketgeedong the day the stallion arrived.

The shed had cut-out, all the wool had been delivered to the railway trucks, and we were making our last journey home in the evening. Suddenly the mares began to grow restless. They were very tired, and they had been plodding along listlessly in the dust, but now they began tossing the harness about on their immense shoulders and flinging up their heads. One of the leaders quickened her pace, neighing loudly, and the empty wagon began to bump and rattle over the ruts in the track. We were still a long way off but they had scented the stallion who had been placed in one of the yards beside the wool shed. He was standing there majestically, very well aware of the mares, and he elaborately turned his back on them. We covered the last quarter of a mile at a trot, and the mares were barely manageable as we fought to get the collars off their necks. Then, directly they were free, they trotted off to the yard. One after another with an absurd gargantuan grace they came prancing up to the stallion, peered at him closely from a foot or two away, and then, overtaken by some sudden constricting modesty, half turned away and stood waiting. The stallion ignored them. He kept shifting his ground so as to hold himself apart. Then suddenly the stampede began. The stallion came first. He lifted up his

Information Service Australia House, London

Kangaroos on the run

shaggy forelegs and came out of the yard at full gallop
with the twelve mares close behind him; and all the hard
ground round the wool shed shuddered as though a troop
of tanks were going by.

They headed for a low ridge of hills across the plains,
and although the light was failing we could see them quite
distinctly for a while. Pretty soon they spread out in a line
and when they gained the ridge they made a long, black,
silhouetted frieze with their heads up and their manes
flying; and in that dry hot air their neighings and bellow-
ings sounded across to us at the wool shed, clearly and
outlandishly, from half a mile away. The stallion was still
leading, but one or two of the younger mares were gaining
on him, though whether or not this was because he had
slackened his pace a little it was impossible to say. We
lost sight of them at last as they dropped below the ridge.

All that night there were sounds of the horses shuffling
about in the darkness round the camp. But in the morning
they were all there, quietly cropping the grass together,
and when we called them they came up very obediently
in the usual way. We had no difficulty in getting the
harness on to the mares, and the stallion went back to the
stud.

Of all this, no more at Cocketgeedong. They run the
wool to the railway now in Diesel trucks.

But perhaps there is a rough justice here, or at any rate
a discernible logic. It is the imported domestic animals, the
horse, the sheep, and the cattle, which have driven the
wild creatures of Australia off their prehistoric feeding
grounds and hastened their extinction; and now presumably the domestic animals themselves will gradually
die out until man is left alone with his machines on the
barren earth.

Yet once you have been to Australia it is impossible not
to develop a protective and kindly feeling for the wild life
there, the bright cockatoos, the lizards, the kangaroos,

and the penguins. Not very many of them are destined to survive the next hundred years or so in the new jungle of atomic piles and uranium workshops. Of them all I must confess that the poor empty-headed koala bear is my hero. He is, indeed, my albatross, for I do have one story about him, and like the Ancient Mariner I have detained you, perhaps unconsciously, in order to tell it.

One day on Phillip Island we decided to catch a bear. We were very young and I suppose we were bored that day. At all events, it seemed to be an amusing thing to do, and it was not long before we found one in a clump of gums. He was a young bear, relatively agile, and there was nothing we could do with sticks or by throwing stones to loosen his grip on the tree. He cried out and retreated to the topmost branches. Eventually I went up the tree after him, and he watched me coming. My object was to shake the branches until he fell, and he knew there was no retreat. However, he made one last effort. The branches of the neighbouring gum trees were only three or four feet away. He jumped with his arms flung out and actually succeeded in clutching at a handful of leaves; but they were not strong enough to hold him. He whimpered in terror for a moment, and then, while we yelled in triumph, he crashed down to the ground and landed with a heavy thump.

Although all this happened twenty-five years ago, I remember that bear very well, the way he cried and how he fell. He was already dead when we reached him, and we buried him quickly under the trees with the bunch of gum leaves still clutched in his claws. So far as I know no one ever found out about it. Just my sense of guilt remains.